AN UNOFFICIAL GUIDE TO
BATTLE ROYALE

EXPERT SECRETS TO ISLAND TRAVEL FOR FORTNITERS

MASTER COMBAT SERIES #2

JASON R. RICH

Sky Pony Press
New York

Sky Pony Press books may be purchased in bulk at special discounts for sales promotion, corporate gifts, fund-raising, or educational purposes. Special editions can also be created to specifications. For details, contact the Special Sales Department, Sky Pony Press, 307 West 36th Street, 11th Floor, New York, NY 10018 or info@skyhorsepublishing.com.

Sky Pony® is a registered trademark of Skyhorse Publishing, Inc.®, a Delaware corporation.

Visit our website at www.skyponypress.com.

Authors, books, and more at SkyPonyPressBlog.com.

10 9 8 7 6 5 4 3 2 1

Library of Congress Cataloging-in-Publication Data is available on file.

Cover design by Brian Peterson
Cover artwork by Getty Images
Interior photography by Jason R. Rich

Print ISBN: 978-1-5107-4972-6
E-Book ISBN: 978-1-5107-4977-1

Printed in the United States of America

TABLE OF CONTENTS

SECTION 1

FORTNITE: BATTLE ROYALE— GET READY TO FIGHT!

Are you ready to do some exploration? Are you cunning enough to avoid the deadly storm and seek out and then pummel your enemies while showing absolutely no mercy? As soon as your soldier gets transported to the mysterious island where each match takes place, these will be some of your most pressing responsibilities.

Get ready to experience Fortnite: Battle Royale—*one of the most popular games in the world. Whether you play this mega-popular game on your PC, Mac, Xbox One, PlayStation 4, Nintendo Switch, iPhone, iPad, or Android-based mobile device, you're going to put your gaming skills to the test!*

One of the great things about this game is that it's constantly evolving. Literally every week, there are a new types of weapons, loot items, vehicles, game play elements, and/or game play modes added to Fortnite: Battle Royale *that'll keep you challenged, even if you consider yourself to be a pro.*

Each of the different game play modes provide different challenges and fighting scenarios—some that you'll face alone, others that you can experience with one partner, and some that you'll delve into as a member of a four-person squad. There are also team-based game play modes that divide up all of the soldiers into two 25- or 50-person teams that must compete to accomplish specific objectives during a match.

First Choose a Game Play Mode

Whenever you launch Fortnite: Battle Royale, *from this Select Game Mode screen, you're asked to choose between the* **Save the World**, **Battle Royale**, *or* **Creative** *game play modes.*

Save the World is a cooperative, Player versus Environment mode that follows a detailed storyline. While it's still a combat game, it's very different from the various **Battle Royale** modes that are continuously offered. Originally, Epic Games charged gamers up to $39.99 (US) to unlock the Save the World campaign, but it's expected that the price will drop to free sometime soon. Of course, *Fortnite: Battle Royale* always has been and continues to be a free game (but with optional in-game purchases available).

The **Creative** gaming mode allows you to fully customize the mysterious island from scratch and create your very own rules of engagement for matches. Experience your creation on your own or invite your online friends who are up for the challenge.

Every day, Epic Games features a different selection of gamer-created matches that anyone can experience. What you'll discover when playing matches created using the **Creative** gaming mode is that weapons, loot items, vehicles, and tools that have been vaulted from the main Fortnite: Battle Royale game play modes are often still available.

When something gets "vaulted," that means that Epic Games has removed it from the main *Fortnite: Battle Royale* game play modes, but the weapon, item, vehicle, or tool could be reintroduced at any time in the future.

*Select the **Battle Royale** option from the Game Mode screen to access the Fortnite: Battle Royale Lobby (shown here). From this screen, you're able to manage many aspects of the game prior to a match and choose which **Battle Royale** game play mode you want to experience.*

*Three of the **Battle Royale** game play modes are always available–**Solo**, **Duos**, and **Squads**. From this menu, you're also able to access the **Creative** and **Playground** modes, plus choose to experience the ever-changing selection of temporary game play modes Epic Games offers. For example, there are many variations of **Team Rumbles** (also referred to as **50v50** matches) that divide up 100 gamers into two teams with specific objectives to achieve during a match.*

*All the **Battle Royale** gaming modes have one thing in common. During a match, you'll compete against up to 99 other soldiers, each controlled in real time by a different gamer. The main objective is to become the last soldier, team, or squad alive on the island at the end of the match. There's no second or third place. You either win #1 Victory Royale, or your soldier perishes.*

A **Solo** match involves you controlling one soldier who lands on the island in conjunction with up to 99 other soldiers (each controlled by a separate gamer). The goal is to achieve #1 Victory Royale by becoming the last person alive at the end of the match. Everyone else needs to be eliminated.

When you experience a **Duos** match, you and a partner team up to defeat the other 98 soldiers on the island, each of whom kicks off the match with a partner of their own. You can partner up with someone you know (an online friend) or have the game match you up with a stranger.

To experience a Duos match with an online friend, choose the Don't Fill option from the game play mode menu screen after selecting the Duos option. Once you've selected the Don't Fill option, return to the Lobby, select one of the "+" slots displayed on either side of your soldier near the center of the screen, and then invite one of your online friends to join you.

A **Squads** match allows you to team up with three other gamers (either your online friends or strangers). The four of you will work together to defeat the other 24 squads that join your match. The goal is for you to help keep yourself and your squad mates alive, while eliminating others from the match. Only one gamer (or one squad) will earn the #1 Victory Royale title at the end of the match. Everyone else will perish.

Just like when experiencing Duos mode, when you participate in a Squads match, you can have the game randomly select your squad mates (by choosing the Fill option) or choose them yourself from your online friends (by first choosing the Don't Fill option).

The Island Map Is Constantly Changing

Every ninety days or so, Epic Games kicks off a new gaming season. At the same time, major changes are made to the island map, where the matches take place.

If you've been playing *Fortnite: Battle Royale* for a while, you've seen all sorts of disasters occur on the island, resulting in points of interest (locations) being destroyed or dramatically altered, while new points of interest, with vastly different types of terrain, are introduced. There have been earthquakes, massive explosions, volcano eruptions, meteor strikes, invasions, toxic radioactive explosions, an ice age, and other terrain-changing disasters.

The specific locations on the map offer different types of terrain. As you explore, you'll encounter wide open and flat areas. In this situation, you'll want to run (not walk) in a zigzag pattern and keep jumping up and down in order to make yourself a fast-moving target that's difficult to hit.

In order to survive during a match, it's important to always be mindful of your surroundings and discover unexpected and strategic ways to use the terrain around you to your tactical advantage.

Some terrain will include hills, mountains, lakes, rivers, valleys, or desert areas. Within many of these locations a few small structures (which are often worth searching) will often be scattered around.

Many areas contain single-family homes or smaller buildings.

Battles and firefights can take place anywhere on the island—outdoors, within any building or structure on the island, or in and around structures and fortresses that soldiers build themselves during matches.

Within a few areas, you'll encounter multi-story buildings positioned closely together. During your exploration, you'll also come across farmhouses, stables, mining tunnels, mansions, factories, tall watchtowers, storage container facilities, research facilities, explorer outposts, junk yards, grave yards, stone crypts, secret bases, indoor sporting complexes, camping lodges, and many other types of structures.

Anytime you're out in the open, use surrounding objects, such as trees, rock formations, or bushes (shown here) to provide a hiding place when needed. While solid objects will provide some defensive protection against attacks, a bush will not. A bush can only keep your soldier out of sight. There is a soldier hiding in this bush. If you choose to hide your soldier within a bush, keep their weapon drawn and ready to shoot, in case an enemy gets too close. Should your location be discovered, be ready to react quickly.

Regardless of which Fortnite: Battle Royale *gaming season you're about to experience, you can be sure you'll encounter an island filled with at least twenty different labeled points of interest on the island map. In between these points of interest are many other areas that you'll want or need to travel through and explore in order to survive and stay clear of the deadly storm. This is what the island map looked like midway through Season 8.*

When viewing the Island Map screen, notice that along the top of the map are the letters "A" through "J," and along the left edge of the map are the numbers "1" through "10." Use these letters and numbers to identify coordinates on the map.

For example, at coordinates D5.5 you'll discover Tilted Towers, one of the most popular points of interest on the island, at least during seasons 1 through 8. Coordinates F3 is where Lazy Lagoon is currently located. While looking at the Island Map screen, you can zoom in and out, plus scroll around using the Zoom feature. Tilted Towers was recently destroyed. In its place, a new and futuristic city, called Neo Tilted, was built. The fighting and survival strategies used in any city on the island will be similar.

When you play a Solo match, a small white triangle icon is used to show your soldier's current location on the map. Different colored triangle icons are used to show the location(s) of your partner or squad mates. A soldier's location icon is seen here near the volcano near map coordinates H3.

If you're playing a Duos or Squads match, and you want to create a rendezvous point, whether as a desired landing spot or a meetup place during a match, mark it on the map by placing a Marker.

Once you place a Marker on the island map, a colored flare is displayed on the main game screen that can be seen from a distance—either while you're freefalling toward land at the start of a match, or anytime during a match.

Keep in mind, while you can use the island map to keep tabs on your partner, squad mates, or teammates (if you're playing a 50v50 match, for example), you'll never see the locations of your enemies or the Markers they've placed on the map. Likewise, your enemies won't be able to see your Markers.

Watch Out for the Deadly Storm!

Just one of the many things you'll need to contend with each time you visit the island is the deadly storm. It forms shortly after a match begins and then slowly expands, making more of the island uninhabitable as the match progresses. The storm forces the soldiers who remain alive to get closer and closer together, until everyone is forced to fight for their own survival. While exploring the island, the storm looks like a blue wall. Stay on the clear side of the wall to remain safe.

For every second your soldier spends on the wrong side of the blue wall, a portion of their Health meter is depleted. Spending too long in the storm will cause your soldier to be eliminated from the match.

When viewing the main game screen, the mini-map shows you when the storm is close by or closing in. The storm-filled area is displayed in pink. When a white line appears within the mini-map, this shows the path to follow to avoid the storm as it expands and moves.

At any time during a match, check the island map to see the uninhabitable areas of the island. When one circle is displayed on the map, the space inside it represents the safe area.

Whenever two circles are displayed on the map, the outer circle shows you the currently safe area of the island. The inner circle shows where the safe area will be the next time the storm expands and moves.

A timer can be found directly below the mini-map on the main game screen. It tells you when the storm will be expanding and moving again. You'll also periodically see warning messages appear in the center of the screen, so pay attention. By checking the timer and the island map, you can determine where you need to travel to next in order to stay in the safe area and figure out how long you have to make it to the safe area.

Keep Tabs on Your Soldier's Health and Shield Meters

Every soldier has Health and Shield meters that contain a certain amount of HP. Likewise, all destroyable objects on the island also have HP meters. Each direct hit with a weapon depletes some of the meter's HP. When a soldier's Health meter hits zero, that soldier is immediately eliminated from the match.

Using Health replenishment items, like Bandages, Med Kits, Slurp Juices, Cozy Campfires, or Chug Jugs, it's possible to replenish some or all of your soldier's health.

To active and then maintain your soldier's Shield meter, you'll need to use a Shield replenishment item, such as a Mushrooms, Small Shield Potions, Shield Potions, or Chug Jugs. Shields will protect your soldier against weapon attacks, but not from injury caused by the storm or falls. The soldier shown here is drinking a Shield Potion. It'll boost his Shields to 50 percent within a few seconds.

At the start of a match, a soldier's Health meter is maxed out at 100HP and their Shield meter is at zero. This is shown at the bottom-center of the screen on most gaming systems. Each time a soldier gets injured, as a result of an attack or fall, for example, some of their Health HP gets depleted. Again, based on which gaming system you're using, where this information is displayed varies.

While every soldier in Fortnite: Battle Royale has a Health meter, just about every structure, building, object, and most vehicles also have an HP (Hit Point) meter. This meter will appear when your soldier faces the object. As you can see, the HP meter for this Quadcrasher vehicle maxes out at 400.

When a structure, building, object, or vehicle's HP meter is full, the meter will be solid green and display its total number of Hit Points. If the item gets damaged, as a result of weapon fire or an explosion, for example, its HP meter will diminish. As soon as an HP meter reaches zero, that structure, building, object, or vehicle will be destroyed and disappear. Here, the brick wall's HP meter is down to 30 out of 300. It needs to be repaired quickly, or it'll be destroyed with one or two more bullet hits.

Structures that are built by soldiers can be repaired once they're damaged (but before a building tile's HP meter hits zero). Other objects and items, including vehicles, cannot be repaired. Not all vehicles can be damaged, however. Shown here, the brick wall is being repaired. You can see green "+" symbols on the screen which indicate the repair is in progress. The wall's HP meter is also slowly increasing.

You'll Be Required to Explore the Island During Each Match

The deadly storm expands and moves randomly during each match. So, depending on your chosen landing location after freefalling from the Battle Bus at the start of a match, within a few minutes, you could find yourself needing to travel a great distance in order to stay within the safe area, or you could discover you're already in the safe area—at least until the storm expands and moves again.

If you choose to land on the outskirts of the island, in a remote location and the storm randomly forms on the same side of the island, you'll find yourself having to travel a far distance quickly to outpace the storm.

As each match progresses, the safe area will get smaller and smaller, until all remaining soldiers are very close together. In fact, some End Games (the last few minutes of a match) take place with the remaining soldiers literally on top of each other within a single building, fortress, or structure.

When choosing a landing spot at the start of the match, selecting somewhere near the center of the island reduces your chances of having to travel great distances to outrun the storm.

At the start of a match, the Battle Bus delivers all one hundred soldiers from the pre-deployment area to the island. This is a one-way trip, and the flying blue bus never actually lands on the island. Instead, each soldier needs to choose the ideal time to leap from the Battle Bus and freefall toward their desired landing spot.

While in the pre-deployment area, or during the first minute or two your soldier is aboard the Battle Bus, check the island map to determine the random route the bus will take over the island. The line that's made up of small arrows shows you the starting and ending points of the route, as well as the direction the Battle Bus will travel.

During your soldier's freefall, use the directional controls to navigate toward the desired landing spot. Point your soldier downward to fall faster.

Use the random route of the Battle Bus to help you choose your desired landing location. Then, at the appropriate moment, use the Jump command to make your soldier leap from the bus and begin their freefall.

As you'll discover, if you plan to land in a popular location, the soldier who reaches the landing spot first and grabs a weapon will be at a major advantage. Those who follow run the risk of being shot and eliminated from the match within seconds after landing. While airborne, you can navigate and often soar through the air across at least half the length of the island.

Choose Your Landing Location Wisely

The landing location you choose will determine a few important things that'll impact your experience during that match.

Choosing to land in the heart of a popular location will typically mean that within moments of reaching the island, your soldier will encounter enemies. Thus, you can expect to engage in firefights almost immediately.

Knowing that you may need to fight right away, as soon as your soldier lands, your first and most important task is to find and grab a weapon (and ammo) so your soldier can defend themselves or attack anyone who poses a threat.

For less experienced gamers, another approach is to choose a landing location that's more remote and less popular. As a result, you'll typically have more time to explore the area and build up a proper arsenal before having to engage in firefights.

Keep in mind: upon landing you won't always see enemies, even ones who are in very close proximity. If you're able to find cover, take a moment to listen carefully for the sounds enemies make—like footsteps, weapon fire, sounds generated by building, doors opening or closing, or the sound of nearby vehicles.

As you analyze the island map and consider the route the Battle Bus will take, know that many gamers opt to leap from the bus at the very start of the route (in this case over Sunny Steps), while some wait until the very last possible second to depart from the bus when it reaches the end of its route (in this case near Happy Hamlet).

Since almost every possible route that the bus can take goes either directly over the center of the island or close to it, points of interest near the center of the map (such as Neo Tilted, Loot Lake, and Dusty Divot) tend to be popular. As the map changes with new game updates, the points of interest near the map's center will always be popular landing spots, regardless of what they're called.

Each gaming season, Epic Games introduces new points of interest to the map. These too tend to be extremely popular, especially during the first few weeks of a new season. If you choose to land at one of these locations, it's likely to be populated with a bunch of enemies whom you'll encounter quickly—sometimes within seconds after landing.

There's a tall wooden tower near Lonely Landing, for example, where you'll often find a chest and plenty of goodies to grab.

Near the top of the wooden tower you'll often discover a chest, along with other useful items lying on the ground. What's in the chest will help you quickly build up your soldier's arsenal.

One of the worst mistakes you can make is landing in the heart of a popular point of interest with no plan whatsoever. If you don't know exactly where to go to discover a chest or weapon stash, you'll likely get shot within seconds of landing.

Upon choosing one of these more remote and less popular locations (which will give you extra time to explore and build your soldier's arsenal), start grabbing what you need, but refer to the map after a few minutes once the storm forms, to determine where the first safe region will be. As you can see here, the soldier has 1 minute and 43 seconds to travel into what will be the safe zone once the storm expands and moves.

As you study the island map, you'll discover plenty of unlabeled locations on the island that are remote, but offer random, stand-alone structures in which you'll often find chests, as well as weapons, ammo, and loot items lying on the ground.

The drawback to landing in a very remote section of the island is that your soldier may need to travel a great distance within the first few minutes of the match to stay within the safe area. However, during this travel, your soldier will potentially be well armed and prepared for enemy encounters. Using a vehicle or another transportation option will help your soldier travel faster around the island.

Whenever you need to help your soldier travel a far distance in order to outrun the storm, look for a nearby zipline that points in the right direction, or find a vehicle that'll take you just about anywhere you want or need to go.

Prepare for a Safe Landing

Once you've chosen a landing location, determine the best moment for your soldier to leap from the Battle Bus and begin their freefall.

While still on the Battle Bus, use the directional controls to see the back end of the bus. You'll be able to see when other soldiers make their leap. By waiting for a moment when few soldiers are simultaneously leaving the bus, you're less apt to encounter those enemies immediately upon landing.

During freefall, use your directional controls to help your soldier glide through the air toward the desired landing spot. If you point the soldier straight downward, he or she will fall faster. Being the first to land at a desired spot, particularly one that's popular, is extremely important. The first soldier to land at a specific location has more time to grab nearby weapons and then start shooting at enemies as they land after your soldier.

Regardless of when your soldier leaps from the Battle Bus, he or she should be able to glide in midair and cover almost half of the island before landing, if necessary. You can increase the distance your soldier is able to travel by activating their Glider early, which slows their rate of descent and gives you increased navigational control. However, this is best done only if you're fairly certain you'll be the only soldier landing at the desired landing spot, since it'll take you longer to get there.

To help guide you to your desired landing location when playing a Solo match, or to help your partner or squad mates see a designated rendezvous location, place a Marker on the map. Each gamer has their own colored Marker for easy identification. Anytime you place a Marker on the map, only you and your partner or squad mates can see it. Markers are not seen by rivals.

Once a Marker is placed on the map, it can be seen by you and your partner or squad mates from a distance. This makes it easier to navigate directly to the exact location that's been marked. The blue flare coming from the island is the Marker created by the gamer controlling this soldier.

As your soldier begins approaching land, to ensure a safe landing, their Glider automatically deploys. Again, this gives you greater navigational control during those final moments of descent.

Be sure to study the land as your soldier is approaching. If you notice other soldiers landing nearby, veer in another direction to put distance between you and the enemy if they'll be landing first and be able to grab a weapon before your soldier.

Most houses have an attic, and within the attic, you'll often discover a chest that'll contain useful weapons, ammo, and/ or loot. Knowing this, it's faster to land directly on the roof of a house, smash through the roof using your soldier's Harvesting Tool, and then jump down into the attic.

Another decision you'll need to make when choosing an exact landing spot is whether you want to land on the ground, on top of an object, or on the roof of a building, house, or structure. Shown here, a soldier has landed on the ground, out in the open, but close to a small farm house (near Paradise Palms close to map coordinates I9) that will hopefully contain at least one weapon and some ammo.

The alternative is to land on the ground outside of a house, enter the house through a door, climb up the stairs, build a ramp that'll allow your soldier to reach the attic, and then use the soldier's Harvesting Tool to smash through the ceiling. This option takes longer. However, as you make your way through the house, grab weapons, ammo, and loot items that are lying out in the open, on the floor. Notice that the soldier was already able to grab a weapon that was located on the ground floor of the house.

Always avoid landing in a wide-open space, such as a field. Doing so makes you an easy target for a sniper or any enemy with a mid- to long-range weapon to spot and shoot, since there will be no place for your soldier to take cover. Remember, if you don't yet have any resources (wood, stone, or metal), you can't build, either.

When choosing a landing spot, if you notice a mountain, hill, or rooftop that has a chest on top, it might make sense to land on the top of that elevation. Look for the golden glow of a chest during the final moments of your soldier's freefall. By landing on a hill or mountain and being able to quickly grab a weapon, you gain a potential height advantage over any enemies below, so you can look down and shoot at your targets. If there's no weapon to be seen before landing, choose another location.

On this mountaintop, there was a chest that could be seen before landing, and also a Hoverboard, so the soldier could easily and quickly make her way off of the mountain and continue her exploration.

Yet another option when choosing a landing spot is to find a small hut or structure that's near, but not directly inside, a popular point of interest. This one is on the outskirts of Neo Tilted. Once you grab a weapon, you can shoot at enemies below, or make your way into this very popular urban area of the island.

Just a few steps away from the hut on top of the mountain that overlooks Neo Tilted is this RV with a trailer. During this match, sitting on the trailer is a vehicle that your soldier can hop into and drive. The location of vehicles on the island is not consistent from match to match. You seldom know where they'll spawn (appear).

Doing this allows you to land, quickly grab a weapon, and then travel into the point of interest once you're armed and ready for battle. The slight delay it'll take you to reach the point of interest might give other soldiers time to pick clean the weapons, ammo, and loot items in the area, but if you're able to defeat those enemies during firefights, you'll be able to grab the items you want that they leave behind after they've been eliminated from the match.

Once your soldier is riding in a vehicle, he or she can head directly into Tilted Towers, or quickly travel to whatever destination you choose. Tilted Towers is now called Neo Tilted, and it looks a lot different, although it's still the largest city on the island.

One of the best ways to choose perfect landing spots is to get to know the terrain and remember what you experienced during past matches or while watching other gamers. Many objects, including chests, respawn in the same location for each match, and the layout of buildings and structures only changes as a result of game updates made by Epic Games.

Consider where you've been in the past and try to recall exactly what you encountered there. Your past experiences and exploration of the island will help you make more intelligent landing spot decisions in the future.

Each Method of Transportation Offers Pros and Cons

Your soldier's primary way of traveling around the island is on foot. Using your keyboard/mouse or controller, you can make your soldier walk, run, crouch down, tiptoe, or jump in any direction. Here, the soldier is stuck within the storm and is running toward the safe zone.

Any time your soldier crouches down and tiptoes, he or she will generate very little noise, but this is a lot slower than walking or running. In this case, the soldier needed to crouch down to pass under the half-open garage door.

Unfortunately, even running at top speed, often isn't fast enough to outrun the storm if your soldier gets caught in it, or if he or she needs to quickly retreat from an attack.

The good news is that at any given time, there are multiple ways to quickly travel around the island, although the options change with each new gaming season. Shown here are a few examples. The main focus of this guide is on how to travel around the island using various types of vehicles, loot items, and the island's natural phenomena (like Rifts and Geysers).

As you'll discover, each transportation method offers pros and cons, especially if you're playing a Duos or Squads match and you want two or more soldiers to travel together. The Hoverboard, for example, is an ideal, one-soldier vehicle. It allows you to travel fast across any type of terrain. It's also extremely maneuverable, but it leaves your soldier vulnerable to attacks if an enemy starts shooting.

Your Adventure Begins in the Lobby

Prior to each match, you'll find yourself in the Fortnite: Battle Royale **Lobby**. Your soldier, dressed in his or her currently selected outfit, can be seen in the center of the screen. Along the top-center of the screen are eight tabs. They're labeled Lobby, Battle Pass, Challenges, Events, Locker, Item Shop, Career, and Store. (These options may vary after Season 8.) You can also access the game's Settings menus, choose a game play mode, invite online friends to join you in a match, view Challenges, and access other gaming features from the Lobby.

Battle Pass–_Choose this option to purchase a new Battle Pass during a gaming season, to view each Tier of a Battle Pass and see the prize that's awarded for completing the tier-based challenge, or to purchase and unlock individual Tiers. Here, the player is about to purchase a Battle Pass for Season 8 by clicking on the Purchase button._

Once a Battle Pass has been purchased, click on the Purchase Tier button to purchase and unlock one Tier at a time for 150 V-Bucks each.

Challenges–_View daily, weekly, Style, and Event-based Challenges that you can attempt to complete while participating in matches in order to unlock prizes._

Completing a **Style Challenge** allows you to unlock variations of specific outfits that you've previously purchased or unlocked within the game. Not all outfits have multiple styles.

Events—Discover a selection of daily or weekly events or competitions that you can participate in. Some are open to everyone, while others need to be unlocked first.

Locker—It's from here you're able to customize the appearance of your soldier by choosing an outfit, Back Bling (backpack) design, Harvesting Tool design, Glider design, Contrail design, up to six emotes, and up to six weapon/vehicle wraps. You're also able to select a custom Banner design, background music, and Loading Screen graphic.

Items available from the Locker must first be purchased (using V-Bucks, which can be acquired using real money), or unlocked. Once you purchase or unlock an item, it's yours forever and gets stored within the Locker.

There are hundreds of different outfits, gear-related items, emotes, and wraps to purchase or unlock, and new items are introduced every day. By mixing and matching outfits with gear-related items, it's possible to make your soldier look truly unique. However, all customizations are for cosmetic purposes only. These do not impact your soldier's in-game capabilities in anyway whatsoever. The outfits shown here have already been purchased or unlocked and are stored within the Locker.

Item Shop–*Every day, a new collection of outfits, gear-related items, and/or Emotes is made available for sale exclusively from the Item Shop. Purchases are made using V-Bucks (in-game currency). On the left side of the Item Shop, below the Featured Items heading, are a selection of outfits and items that are being highlighted that day.*

The items displayed below the Featured Items heading tend to be ranked as Epic or Legendary. They typically cost between 1,500 and 2,000 V-Bucks each and will only be available for a limited time. These items may never be re-released again. Depending on how large of a V-Bucks bundle you purchase at once, 1,500 V-Bucks is equivalent to around $15.00 (US) and 2,000 V-Bucks is equivalent to around $20.00 (US).

Shown here is the Global Wins Leaderboard, which you can access from the Career menu. This Leaderboard displays the top Fortnite: Battle Royale gamers in the world and is updated continuously.

Displayed on the right side of the Item Shop, below the Daily Items heading, is a selection of six additional outfits, gear-related items, and/or emotes, each sold separately. These tend to be ranked as Common, Uncommon, Rare, or Epic items. They'll be made available on a specific day but will reappear within the Item Shop every few weeks or months.

There are several independent websites, like FortniteSkins.net (https://fortniteskins.net/outfits), that keep track of all outfits released, as well as when and if each has been rereleased.

*It's from the **Store** that you purchase bundles of V-Bucks using real money. As you can see, a bundle of 1,000 V-Bucks costs $9.99 (US). A bundle of 2,800 V-Bucks is priced at $24.99, while 5,000 V-Bucks are priced at $39.99 (US). If you want to purchase 13,500 V-Bucks at once, it'll cost you $99.99 (US).*

__Career—__Click on the Profile, Leaderboards, or Replays button to see details about your player Profile, top Fortnite: Battle Royale players (on the Leaderboards), or to replay matches or battles you've previously recorded.

At least once or twice per gaming season Epic Games releases a special pack that includes an exclusive outfit, a bundle of 600 V-Bucks, and one or two other items for a flat fee of $4.99 (US). The outfit offered as part of a pack is not available from the Item Shop and will not be rereleased after the current gaming season ends.

Another way to acquire exclusive, limited-edition outfits and other items is to obtain a free Twitch Prime Pack. Epic Games has teamed up with Twitch.tv and Amazon Prime to periodically offer these free item packs.

To obtain a Twitch Prime Pack (when they're available), you'll need to have a free Twitch.tv account that is linked to your Epic Games gaming account, and also be a paid Amazon Prime subscriber. To learn more, visit: www.twitch.tv/prime.

Displayed along the left side of the Lobby screen is information about your Player Level, your Battle Pass Tier (if applicable), and a listing of Suggested Challenges. If there's an important announcement from Epic Games, it'll be displayed at the bottom-center of the screen.

To access the game's Menu, access the Menu icon in the top-right corner of the screen, and then select the gear-shaped Settings Menu icon.

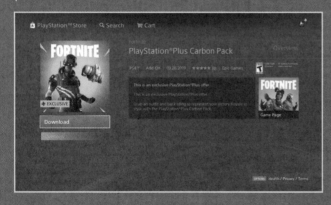

From the PlayStation Store (for PS4 gamers only), Sony occasionally offers exclusive free outfits that you can download and add to your Locker. When visiting the PlayStation Store directly from your PS4, select the Add-Ons category, followed by the Add-Ons for Free subcategory. Choose the Fortnite option, and then select the latest Add-On (as opposed to an Avatar) that's listed. When free outfits are made available, it's only for a limited time.

Customize Your Gaming Experience Before a Match

After you've customized the appearance of your soldier from the Locker access the Game menu to click on the gear-shaped Settings menu icon. From here, you can access a variety of Settings submenus, including: Video (PC and Mac only), Game, Brightness, Audio, Accessibility, Input, Wireless Controller, and Account.

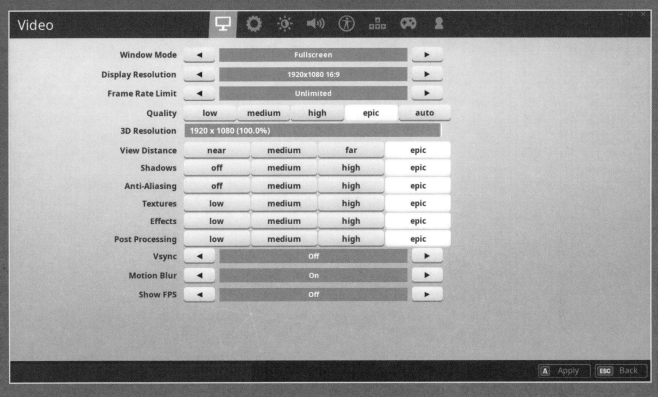

To maximize the speed and quality of the game's graphics when playing Fortnite: Battle Royale on a PC or Mac, for example, you may want to adjust the Display Resolution and other options found within the Video menu. (Shown here on a PC.)

Your accuracy when aiming weapons and the control you'll have over your soldier will depend, in part, on how you adjust the Keyboard/Mouse or Controller sensitivity controls related to the game. Depending on whether you're playing Fortnite: Battle Royale on a computer, console-based system (Xbox One, PS4, or Nintendo Switch), or on a mobile device, the options available from the Game submenu will vary. For example, on the left, the PS4 version of the menu is displayed. On the right is the PC version.

Sound effects play an extremely important role in *Fortnite: Battle Royale*. For this reason, you definitely want to experience the game while wearing quality headphones. However, if you'll be playing any of the game play modes that require you to interact with a partner or squad mates, you'll benefit greatly by connecting a good quality gaming headset with a built-in microphone to your gaming system or computer.

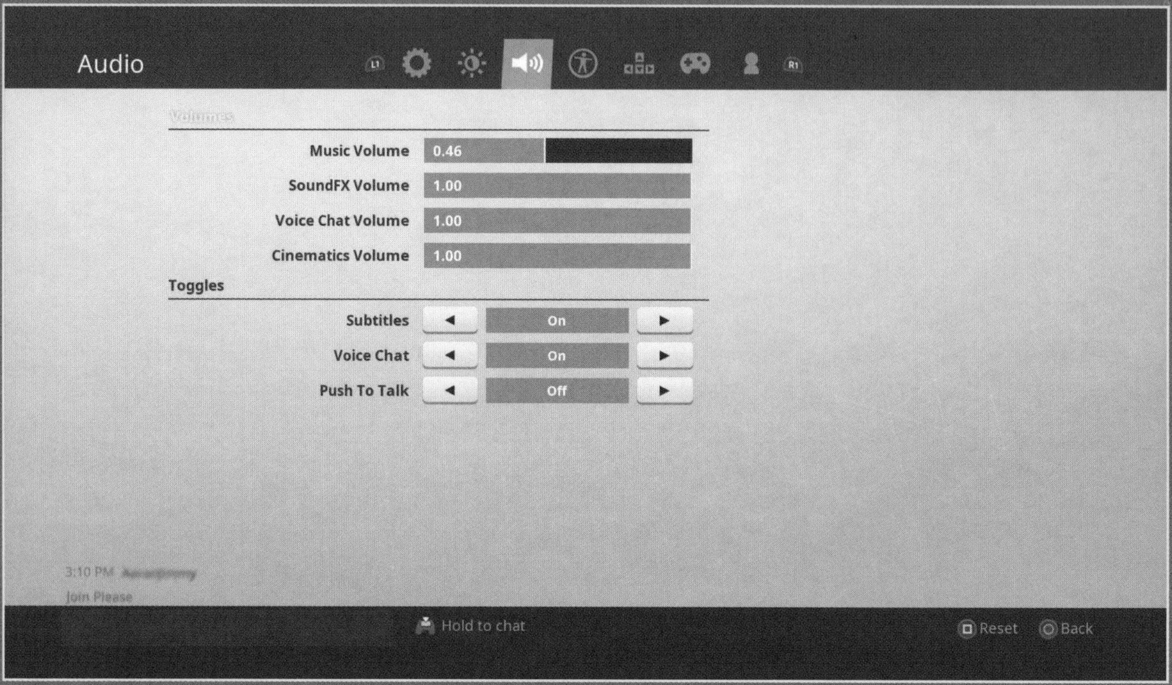

Audio

Volumes		
Music Volume	0.46	
SoundFX Volume	1.00	
Voice Chat Volume	1.00	
Cinematics Volume	1.00	

Toggles

Subtitles	◄	On	►
Voice Chat	◄	On	►
Push To Talk	◄	Off	►

3:10 PM
Join Please

🎤 Hold to chat   □ Reset ◎ Back

From the Settings menu, select the Audio submenu (shown here on a PS4). Consider turning down the Music Volume option. Some gamers opt to turn off the music altogether. Next, turn up the SoundFX Volume. You want to hear all the game's sound effects clearly. If you'll be using the game's Voice Chat mode to communicate with your partner or squad mates, also turn up the Voice Chat Volume option.

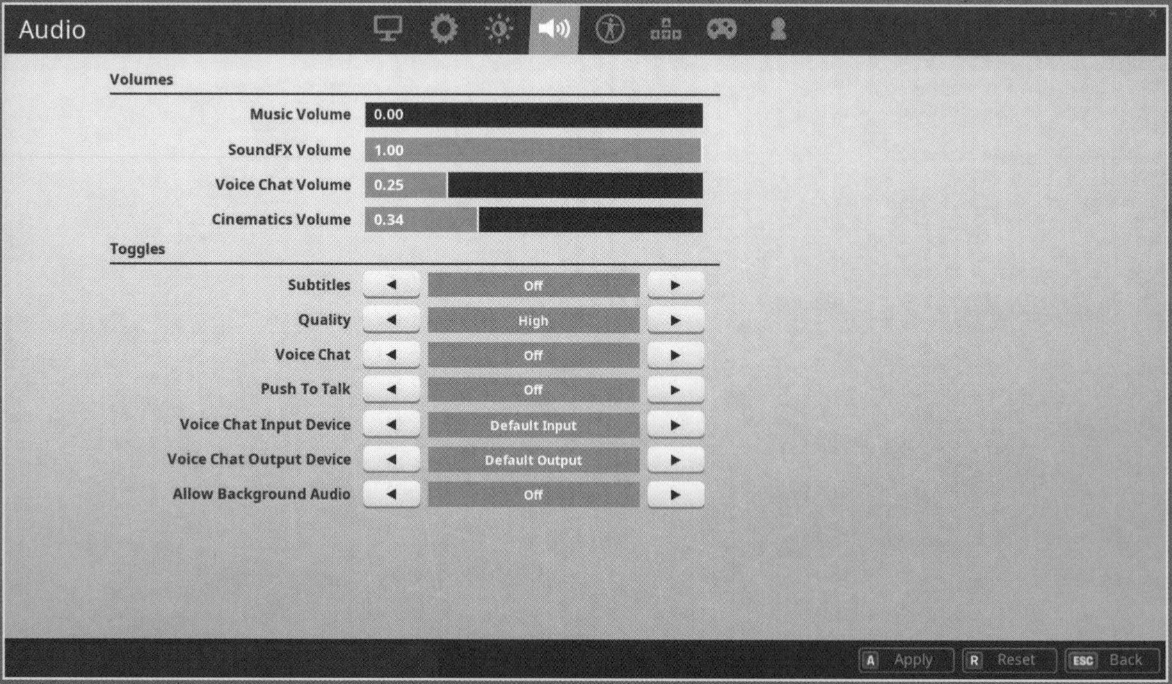

Audio

Volumes		
Music Volume	0.00	
SoundFX Volume	1.00	
Voice Chat Volume	0.25	
Cinematics Volume	0.34	

Toggles

Subtitles	◄	Off	►
Quality	◄	High	►
Voice Chat	◄	Off	►
Push To Talk	◄	Off	►
Voice Chat Input Device	◄	Default Input	►
Voice Chat Output Device	◄	Default Output	►
Allow Background Audio	◄	Off	►

Ⓐ Apply   Ⓡ Reset   ᴱˢᶜ Back

This is the PC version of Fortnite: Battle Royale's *Audio menu.*

There are several different controller layouts to choose from if you access the Controller submenu. Choose one that best fits your personal gaming style and experience level.

Gaming headsets have a built-in microphone. This type of optional accessory is available from a wide range of manufacturers. Some of the more popular gaming headsets used by top-ranked Fortnite: Battle Royale gamers come from companies like Logitech G (www.logitechg.com), HyperX (www.hyperxgaming.com/us/headsets), Razer (www.razer.com/gaming-headsets-and-audio), and Turtle Beach Corp. (www.turtlebeach.com). Shown above is a partial lineup of Logitech G headsets, which range in price from $59.99 (US) to $139.99 (US). These are compatible with PCs, Macs, and all popular console-based gaming systems.

Don't Focus on the Game Settings Used by Top-Ranked Players

Many of the top-ranked Fortnite: Battle Royale gamers publish details about exactly what game equipment they use, as well as the customizations they've made to the various Settings menu and submenu options. While this information is useful for reference, for several reasons, you should not try to replicate another gamer's exact settings.

Depending on whether you're using a keyboard/mouse combo to control the game, or you're using a controller, access the Input or Controller submenu to customize your controls. For example, when using a keyboard/mouse combo, the Input menu allows you to adjust all of the key bindings related to every game feature and command. (Shown here on a PC.)

On the independent Fortnite Base website (https://fortbase.net/pro-players), you can look up the player stats, ranking, gaming equipment list, and game-related settings for many of the best Fortnite: Battle Royale *players in the world. Shown here is the information about Ninja.*

First, unless you have exactly the same gaming equipment and Internet connection speed used by the pro gamer, when you replicate their settings, you'll achieve different results on your own gaming system.

Second, every pro gamer tweaks the game based on their unique gaming style and experience level. If you play using a different style, or your reflexes and game-related muscle memory are not as developed as the pro gamer, copying their game settings will actually be detrimental to your success.

As a newb, you're better off leaving the majority of the *Fortnite: Battle Royale* Settings menu options at their default settings. Then, once you start getting good at playing, tweak the options you believe will improve your game play. Always make small, incremental adjustments to one setting at a time, and then test out how each change works for you by playing one or two matches. Continue to tweak the settings as you deem necessary.

To discover the gaming equipment and customized settings used by top-ranked and pro *Fortnite: Battle Royale* gamers, check out these websites:

- **Best Fortnite Settings**—https://best fortnitesettings.com/best-fortnite -pro-settings
- **Fortnite Base**—https://fortbase.net /pro-players
- **Fortnite Pro Settings & Config**—https: //fortniteconfig.com
- **GamingScan**—www.gamingscan.com /fortnite-competitive-settings-gear
- **ProNettings.net**—https://prosettings.net /best-fortnite-settings-list

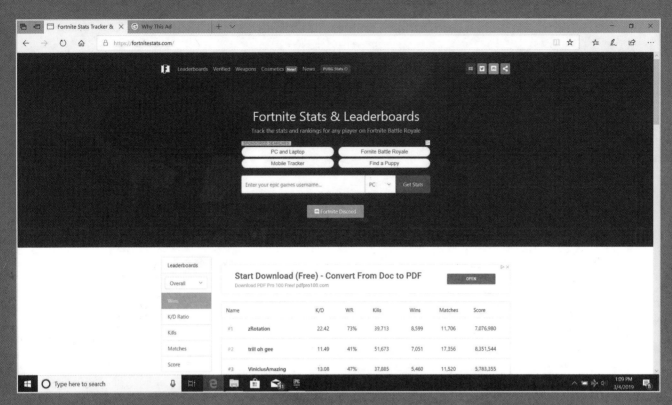

By accessing the free and independent Fortnite Stats & Leaderboard website (https://fortnitestats.com), enter the Epic Games username for any Fortnite: Battle Royale *gamer to see their current stats as a player.*

Prepare to Explore, Fight, Build, . . . and Survive!

During every *Fortnite: Battle Royale* match you participate in, you'll need to juggle a variety of responsibilities, such as:

- Safely exploring the island and traveling between points of interest.
- Avoiding the deadly storm.
- Finding and managing your soldier's arsenal (including weapons, ammo, traps, and explosives)
- Collecting items that'll help with survival.
- Building structures and fortresses.
- Fighting and defeating your enemies.
- Driving in various types of vehicles or using different modes of transportation to get around the island faster.

To successfully handle all these tasks, you'll need to understand the different types of terrain you'll encounter on the island and know how to use your surroundings to your tactical advantage. It's also essential that you keep moving to avoid the storm, launch attacks on enemies, or retreat when necessary, in order to improve your chances of making it into the End Game.

The majority of this unofficial strategy guide's focus is on helping you get comfortable exploring the island using the various transportation options available to you. You'll soon discover how to make the best use of each vehicle type or transportation method in a wide range of situations.

Knowing how to best use these transportation options (and understanding the vulnerabilities each offers) will help you get around faster and stay alive longer during each match you experience.

SECTION 2

USE THE TERRAIN TO YOUR ADVANTAGE

While the names and appearances of the island's various points of interest change on a pretty consistent basis, the types of terrain you'll encounter when exploring the island remain pretty consistent from gaming season to gaming season.

In this section, you'll discover the more common types of terrain you'll travel through when playing *Fortnite: Battle Royale*, plus discover some awesome strategies for using the terrain to your advantage whether it's for tactical, defensive, or exploratory purposes.

For demonstration purposes, many of the screenshots shown in this guide were created using *Fortnite: Battle Royale's* Playground mode on a PS4. The strategies you're about to learn, however, will work in **any game play mode you choose to experience,** on any compatible gaming system.

Buildings and Urban Regions

Since *Fortnite: Battle Royale* first launched, Tilted Towers (located near map coordinates D5.5) has been one of the game's most popular points of interest. Sure, it's changed and evolved over time, but this urban area is filled with tall buildings, streets, and shops, a parking lot, a tall clock tower, and plenty of structures to explore. At any given time, this is just one of the urban areas you'll discover on the island. As you know, Tilted Towers is now called Neo Tilted, and it has a futuristic design.

Urban areas tend to be the most popular on the island, so you're virtually guaranteed to encounter a bunch of enemies right away, so be prepared!

General Strategies for Exploring and Fighting in and Around Buildings

If you choose to land in an urban area, your landing spot should be on the roof of a tall building or structure. Look for the glow of a chest on the roof, or at least the glare or reflection from a weapon that's lying on the roof, out in the open.

You want to be able to land and grab a weapon right away. As you can see here, the soldier was able to grab a Pistol. She's now able to defend herself if an enemy lands right after her, or she encounters rivals as she explores the building she landed on.

When exploring an urban area with tall buildings that are located relatively close to each other, one strategy for survival is to stick to the high ground. Find and grab a long-range weapon and then pick off enemies by peeking out a window from a high-up floor or the roof of a building.

Instead of walking along the roads or sidewalks (on ground level) within a dense urban area where enemies will often be above you, or could attack from any side, consider traveling quickly (and with great maneuverability) using a Hoverboard. Other vehicles can work too. You might not be able to outrun an incoming attack on foot, but you can often maneuver around quickly enough to avoid harm if you're using a vehicle.

If you're riding a Hoverboard in an area with lots of buildings and narrow streets and you attempt to use the Boost feature, you'll have less time to make sharp turns and are more likely to crash into objects or buildings, which will actually slow you down. Ideally, you want to travel as fast as possible, while maintaining control so you can maneuver quickly.

Always be on the lookout for Ammo Boxes. They don't glow or make a sound like chests, but when you open one, you'll be able to stock up on ammo. It's in Ammo Boxes that you'll often find Rockets (which are rarer than other types of ammo).

The guns available on the island use either Light Bullets, Medium Bullets, Heavy Bullets, Shells, or Rockets. If you don't have the right ammo for the guns in your soldier's arsenal, those weapons are useless. Meanwhile, if you run out of ammo during a firefight, or don't swap weapons fast enough, you'll likely wind up getting defeated by your enemy. It's always good to stock up on ammo!

Within many of the buildings, you'll discover chests. As long as it's safe to do so, approach each chest and grab the loot that's inside, so you can build up or improve your soldier's arsenal of weapons and items.

After opening a doorway and passing through, be sure to close the door behind you. An open door is a sure indication someone has been in that area before you. If the door is shut, someone entering after you won't know if you're already inside or not unless they can hear sounds your soldier is making.

Always listen carefully for the sound of footsteps, doors opening and closing, construction noises, and the sound of gunfire. You can often hear enemies approaching before you can see them, especially when you're inside of a building or within a confined space.

As you're exploring a building, crouch down and tiptoe while inside, and always keep your weapon drawn. This will generate much less noise (from footsteps) than walking or running.

By climbing to a higher floor in a building, you can look out of a window and use a Sniper Rifle (or any weapon with a scope) to zoom in on an enemy lurking within another building. You'll often see them by peeking through their building's window.

If you don't see an enemy right away, focus in on a chest, for example. As soon as an enemy approaches the chest to open it, shoot him and try for a headshot.

A headshot always causes more damage than a body shot. Depending on the power and capabilities of the weapon you're using, a single headshot will typically eliminate your adversary.

Anytime you need to travel on street level in a city or urban area, try to avoid being out in the open, in the middle of the street. This makes you an easy target for enemies located above you, as well as those hiding on the ground level in shops or buildings, or behind vehicles or objects.

Whenever it's necessary, crouch down and hide behind solid objects, like walls or broken-down vehicles to shield yourself from enemy attacks. Keep in mind, in an urban area, an attack can come from any direction, including above you.

Avoid getting yourself stuck in a room within a building with no escape plan. In this situation, you'll need to fight your way out. In this case, make sure the door is shut, crouch down behind a solid object (in this case a desk), and aim your weapon at the door. As soon as an enemy tries to enter, start shooting. Just make sure you can't be seen from a window that's behind you or to the sides of you, or a sniper might take you out while you're guarding the door.

Anytime you're within a building and need to fight an enemy, use a close-range weapon, such as any type of Pistol or Shotgun. An SMG (Submachine Gun) can also do mega-damage at close-to-mid range. SMGs are often a weapon of choice for newbs who need a close-range weapon that's more forgiving and versatile.

Remember, you're able to build using different shaped building tiles—either inside or outside. When there's enough space, consider blocking the door with one or two brick or metal walls.

Whenever possible, try to have the height advantage over your opponent. This might mean climbing up on furniture or a staircase, or leaning over a ledge. It's almost always easier to accurately target an enemy that's positioned below you. In this case, the soldier is leaning over a ledge from the second floor of a building. She's crouching down and aiming at the doorway, waiting for an unsuspecting enemy to enter.

Weapon Aiming Tips

When using any weapon, your aim improves dramatically if your soldier is not moving and is crouching down. You'll still have good aiming accuracy if your soldier is standing upright, but not moving. Whenever your soldier is forced to be in motion and shooting at the same time their aim will be at its worst.

To escape from a closed-in space on a high-up floor within a building, climb through a nearby window or smash the outer wall of a building, and then create a ramp or bridge to help you reach safety.

Most types of weapons can be shot "from the hip" (meaning you don't accurately aim by pressing the Aim button on your keyboard or controller). You just point the weapon in the direction of your target and pull the trigger. This allows you to attack or defend yourself faster, but is less accurate than if you aim first.

You'll achieve better aiming accuracy if you press the Aim button before pulling the gun's trigger. (In most cases, when you press the Aim button, you'll also zoom in a bit on your enemy.) The process of aiming takes a tiny bit longer, so it's not always practical, based on the dangers you're facing.

Don't Forget to Use Explosives

Grenades and Dynamite can be tossed through an open window or doorway. If you suspect an enemy is inside of a building, sneak up and peek through a window. Then, toss a few explosive weapons inside. The explosion will typically defeat whomever is inside, plus cause some major damage to the building.

Three Grenades were tossed into the window of this building and after the explosion, a large section of the building itself was demolished.

Never Just Jump Off of a Roof!

Never just leap off of a tall building. If your soldier winds up falling two or three levels, he'll get injured. A fall from more than three levels up will cause him to perish instantly and with a splat. Here's the view from the top of what was the Clock Tower in Tilted Towers. To get back down to ground level, have your soldier smash through the ceiling and drop down. You'll be able to collect weapons from chests, as well as other goodies, on your way down.

Other options for safely reaching ground level include using a Glider item, using Balloons, a Bouncer Pad, or using a Launch Pad, although not all of these items may be available during your match, as various items often get vaulted and then rereleased into the game at a future date. When you go airborne using any of these items, your soldier will not get injured upon landing.

If you've collected a Glider item and you need to jump from a high-up location back to ground level, first select the Glider that's stored in your soldier's inventory. Next, jump up, and while in midair, activate the Glider. Perfect timing is essential! (This maneuver will likely take some practice.) The Glider will activate, and your soldier will be able to soar through the air and make it safely to the ground. While in the air, use the directional controls to navigate. At this point, the Glider works exactly the same way as it does during your soldier's freefall off of the Battle Bus at the start of each match.

In this case, first a brick floor tile was built over the staircase.

Next, a brick pyramid tile was built on top of the floor tile.

Block Off Stairwells After Climbing Up

Once you've climbed up a staircase to reach a higher floor of a building, slow down enemies that may be following you by building walls to block the staircase.

Finally, a brick wall was built as a third blockade to keep enemies from easily following the soldier going into the building.

If you hear an enemy approaching, make your way to a safe location (to avoid possible explosions), crouch down, and get ready for the enemy to breach your barrier. Either that or make a quick exit by building a bridge out of a window, for example.

Build Bridges to Travel Between Buildings

If you need to travel between buildings, instead of going back to ground level, going outside, and walking (or running) on the sidewalk or street, consider building a bridge between rooftops. This allows you to stay high up.

As you're building or crossing the bridge, run (don't walk), since you'll be out in the open and vulnerable.

Assuming you have the resources to spare, consider building walls on either side of your bridge that connects two buildings together. Plus, if there are other buildings that are taller in the area, consider adding a roof to the bridge to protect from overhead attacks.

Here's what the bridge (with walls) looks like from below. It offers pretty good protection when traveling between buildings. Once you cross the bridge, if you don't anticipate needing to make a return trip in the other direction, consider destroying it so that if an enemy wants to follow, they'll need to use their own resources to build their own bridge.

Anytime you're building bridges, ramps, or structures during a *Fortnite: Battle Royale* match, using wood is always the fastest, but it's also the weakest against attacks. Thus, wood is great for ramps and bridges that won't need to withstand gunfire or an explosive attack.

Stone offers more protection and a higher HP per tile than wood, but it's a bit slower to build with. Metal is definitely the strongest building material. It can offer the greatest level of protection against gunfire or an explosive attack, but it's also the slowest to build with.

You could strap on one or two Balloons and leap from rooftop to rooftop, but while airborne you'll travel slowly and the brightly-colored balloons make your solider an easy target to spot. Meanwhile, if a Grappler is available, you can use it to swing from rooftop to rooftop, like Spider-Man®.

Factories and Other Large Structures

Before entering, look and listen for any sign of enemies lurking inside. You can either take cover outside (in this case behind a rock formation) and use a Sniper Rifle (or weapon with a scope) to shoot enemies as they leave, or you can enter with a close-range weapon drawn and be prepared for a firefight inside. An open doorway is a signal that someone has already entered the building or structure, and that he or she could still be inside.

Treat any large factory or structure just as you would any building.

Shown here, a Bolt-Action Sniper Rifle is aimed at the open door. The soldier holding it is waiting for his enemy to leave. As soon as he or she appears within the doorway, the soldier will pull the trigger.

If there's a window you can safely sneak up to, crouch down and approach it to peek inside and look for enemies. In this case, there's a chest just inside the window and the soldier looking through the window is armed with Dynamite. One option is to stay crouched down until an enemy approaches the chest, and then shoot at him or her through the window using a gun. Another option is to stand back away from the window, wait for the enemy to approach the chest, and then toss in two or three sticks of Dynamite. Keep your distance so your soldier doesn't get caught in the explosion. Remember, it takes several seconds for Dynamite to detonate after it's been tossed, so plan accordingly.

Once inside a large structure, it's best to defeat and remove the enemy threat that's inside before you begin looting and exploring. As you approach closed doors, stand to the side before opening them in case an enemy is waiting inside and has their weapon targeted at the door.

You'll likely discover chests within large structures.

If you suspect an enemy is nearby, build metal walls around the chest as needed, so you can safely open it and collect what's inside.

While exploring inside a large building, crouch down and tiptoe so your soldier makes less noise, and be prepared to use nearby objects, such as walls or crates, for cover if someone starts shooting at you.

When you're ready to leave the closed-in area, simply edit one of the metal walls you've built, and add a door.

From a tactical standpoint, it's always better to have a height advantage over your enemies during a firefight.

Farmland

Farmland, regardless of what the point of interest on the map is called, tends to include wide-open areas, crop-filled areas, and scattered buildings—both large and small—that include farmhouses, barns, stables, and silos.

When traveling through dense crops, if you use your soldier's Harvesting Tool (pickaxe), you'll create a path and clear away the crops. This can attract attention, as it makes some noise and causes the crops to disappear.

Simply by walking, running, or crouching down and tiptoeing through the crops, your soldier can remain hidden within them and not attract attention from nearby enemies. The crops can help you hide but offer no protection whatsoever from weapon or explosive attacks.

If you're hiding in the crops, your own visibility will be limited. Consider jumping up periodically to see where you are and where you're headed.

Within many of the buildings and structures found in farmland area, you're apt to discover chests, as well as weapons, ammo, and loot items lying on the ground, out in the open.

Your soldier can crouch down and hide behind haystacks to avoid being seen by enemies, but hay offers zero protection or shielding from bullets. One shot and the haystack will be destroyed, so if you're going to hide behind hay, stay still and be quiet.

Anytime you need to travel across open areas on foot, run (don't walk)! Travel in a zig-zag pattern and jump up periodically to make yourself a moving target. Since there's often nothing to hide behind for protection, be prepared to quickly build a protective wall or mini-fortress if an enemy starts shooting at you.

As always, maintaining a height advantage will help you pick off enemies with better aiming accuracy. For a great view, find the tallest building, object, or structure and get to the top of it. Watch for enemies below. When you're ready to get down, use the Harvesting Tool to smash through the roof or top of the structure, or use a Glider item, Balloons, or similar item that allows for a safe landing.

Anytime you know you're in a safe area, take a few moments to use Health and/or Shield replenishment items to boost your soldier's Health and/or Shield meter, so they'll be ready for the next firefight or battle.

Forests

Forest areas on the island contain lots of tall and often thick trees, growing close to each other. When necessary, crouch down to make yourself a smaller target, and hide behind a tree for protection.

Using the Harvesting Tool to smash trees is a great way to stock up on wood, which can later be used for building ramps, bridges, and structures. Keep an eye on the tree's HP meter. When it reaches zero, the tree disappears and you'll need to harvest another tree if you need more wood.

Harvesting an entire tree (so it disappears) can give away your location if enemies are close by. Instead, keep harvesting the tree until the HP meter gets very low (but does not hit zero) and then move on to the next tree. The tree will remain standing.

One type of Shield replenishment item commonly found in forest areas is Mushrooms. These cannot be picked up, collected, and then used anytime you wish later. Instead, each time you pick up a Mushroom it needs to be consumed immediately. Each Mushroom will replenish your soldier's Shield meter by 5 points.

Keep your eyes peeled when exploring a forest or heavily wooded area. You'll often discover chests on the ground, hidden near tree trucks or rock formations.

If you notice a path through the woods, don't follow it. Newbs tend to follow pathways and roads, which makes them predictable and easy targets. You're better off navigating in between the trees (and being able to hide behind them) as you move through the area.

If you can't climb up a steep hill or mountain on foot, consider using a vehicle or an item, such as Balloons, that'll help you float up into the sky and then land at a desired location.

Hills and Mountains

Rule #1 when it comes to hills and mountains is that you should never leap off of them, unless you have a loot item ready to use that'll help you land safely. Climbing to the top of a hill or mountain gives you that all-important height advantage over your enemies, and gives you a superb view of the surrounding area.

During the End Game if the circle permits, try to reach the top of a hill or mountain and build a fortress on top. This allows you to see enemies approaching from any direction and gives you a height advantage.

Shown here, the soldier is standing on top of their self-built fortress, which is positioned on top of a hill.

When you're on foot, instead of jumping off of a cliff, try sliding down the edge of it. You'll typically land safely.

One way to easily reach the top of a mountain is to build a ramp along its edge. Once you reach the top, consider destroying the ramp, so an enemy can't easily follow you up without using their own resources to build their own ramp.

Another option is to build a ramp upward (or downward) that faces the hill or mountain. This will allow you to reach the top (or bottom) quickly, but while you're on the ramp, it's easy for an enemy to shoot and destroy just one ramp tile near the bottom of the ramp, which will cause the entire ramp to come crashing down with you on it.

Rivers and Lakes

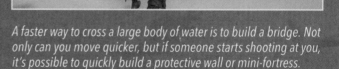

A faster way to cross a large body of water is to build a bridge. Not only can you move quicker, but if someone starts shooting at you, it's possible to quickly build a protective wall or mini-fortress.

The worst thing about traveling through water is that it dramatically slows down your soldier and makes them a wide-open target. If you can avoid crossing through lakes on foot, that's always a good strategy.

Traveling through a shallow stream or river doesn't slow down your soldier too much, but it does leave them out in the open and vulnerable to an attack.

If you absolutely must reach something in the middle of water (such as a Loot Llama that'll likely be chock full of awesome goodies), try to make sure that there are no enemies in the area, and then proceed with extreme caution with your weapon drawn. You won't be able to move fast or build while in the water, but you will be able to shoot back.

Virtually all vehicles can travel through or over water. However, you'll typically move at a slow pace, depending on how deep the water is and the type of vehicle you're driving. Ideally, you want to cross a large body of water on a Hoverboard or use an item that allows you to float above the water. This allows you to travel at the fastest speed and gives you the most maneuverability. In a vehicle, such as the Quadcrasher, if you hit the Boost button repeatedly, you can plow through deep water a bit faster.

When your soldier walks over ice-covered water, their feet will eventually freeze and you'll be able to glide quickly over the ice, but with little navigational control when moving at a fast speed.

When you know there are enemies lurking about, instead of traveling through a body of water, walk around it. This will take longer but keep your soldier from becoming too vulnerable. While on land, you can always hide behind objects, build protective barriers, or launch head-on attacks when you encounter enemies.

Single Family Homes and Mansions

There are multiple regions on the island that offer suburban areas, with clusters of homes located relatively close together.

While you'll likely find weapons, ammo, and loot items lying on the ground, out in the open when exploring homes, the good stuff can often be found in the house's attic or basement.

One way to reach a house's attic is to go inside and make your way to the top floor.

As you travel between labeled points of interest on the map, you're apt to discover individual homes randomly located on the island.

Build a ramp from the floor to the ceiling.

Use your soldier's Harvesting Tool to smash through the ceiling and gain access to the attic.

In many attics (but not all of them) you'll discover a chest, or other things worth grabbing.

Another way to reach a house's attic is to build a ramp from the outside.

To reach the roof of a house from the outside, you can also use an item, such as a Launch Pad, Grappler, or Balloons, that'll help your soldier go airborne. When leaping from the Battle Bus at the start of a match, you can always opt to land on a house's roof.

Once you're on a house's roof, use your Harvesting Tool to smash your way through the roof and jump down into the attic.

Not all houses contain basements. When they do, you can either reach it by going inside and taking the stairs downward, or from the outside by looking for cellar doors on the ground, smashing or shooting open one of the doors, and going inside.

While inside a house, if you encounter enemies, you'll likely need to engage in close-range combat, so have an appropriate weapon ready. The top of a staircase is often a good place to engage an enemy as they're climbing up the stairs.

Before entering a house, look and listen carefully for signs that someone may be inside. For example, if you see the front or back door wide open. Anytime you enter into a house or enter into a room within a house and need to open a door, proceed with caution. You never know what could be waiting on the opposite side.

One way to defeat enemies is to place various types of Traps inside the house, near an entrance or near a staircase, so an enemy will accidently walk into the Trap and activate it before they spot it. Here, a Trap has been placed on the floor and ceiling inside the front door of a house. When someone opens the door and steps inside, the Traps will activate.

Once you've reached the top of a staircase, if you need to slow down someone who is following you, build a metal wall tile to block the staircase.

Remember, from the outside of a house, you can shoot at enemies through windows or an open door. You can also toss explosive weapons, like Grenades, Dynamite, or Clingers, through an open door or window to cause some destruction.

While exploring a house, this is a good time to use the Harvesting Tool to smash objects and collect resources. Smash walls, floors, ceilings, furniture, or appliances.

Anytime you're inside of a house, your soldier will make noise when walking, running, harvesting resources, opening and closing doors, building, or firing a weapon. If someone else is in the house, they'll be able to tell where you are, based on where the noise is coming from.

Don't forget to check inside the garage that's connected to some houses. Occasionally, you'll discover a vehicle parked inside.

Don't forget, you're able to build inside or outside of an existing house, building, or structure. Here, a three-level fortress (made of metal tiles) was built on the roof of a two-story house.

In a suburban area where houses are close together, you can go to the second floor of one house, aim through a window, and then use a Sniper Rifle (or another weapon with a scope) to shoot at enemies coming or going from a nearby house. Aiming for the front door gives you time to position yourself and aim your weapon. Then just wait for the door to open and start shooting whomever is coming or going.

From the top of this fortress, the soldier can look out and see the entire neighborhood.

To travel from one house to another in a suburban area, instead of traveling on ground level, you can maintain the high ground by building a bridge between two homes.

When using a Sniper Rifle (or any weapon with a scope), it's easy to target the door of another house and wait for an enemy to enter or exit so you can shoot them.

Small Structures

Scattered throughout the island, primarily in between the labeled points of interest on the map, you'll find hundreds of small structures.

Some of the small structures you'll encounter are theme-oriented, based on what's happening during the current gaming season of Fortnite: Battle Royale. *This one offers a chest that can be seen from a distance, thanks to its bright golden glow.*

In some small structures, you'll discover weapons, ammo, and/or loot items lying on the ground that you can grab.

Once in a while, you'll discover a chest in one of the small structures. In this case, there was a Vending Machine and a chest inside the small hut.

As you make your way between points of interest, some of these structures offer a good place to rest and hide out for a few minutes, so you can use Health and/or Shield replenishment items with a lower risk of getting attacked while your soldier is vulnerable.

Shown here, the soldier built a metal ramp to cover the doorway of the small structure he chose to hide in.

Once safely inside the stone hut, access your soldier's Inventory screen and move things around in his/her arsenal, if necessary.

Once he was temporarily safe, he took the time to drink a Shield Potion and replenish some of his Shield meter.

Small stone structures located in between points of interest are also good stopping points if you need to access your soldier's Inventory screen and rearrange their arsenal. Once again, these buildings often offer a safe sanctuary. Look for a stone structure (because it's sturdy and can withstand an attack for longer), that has a no windows and just one door. This offers the most protection.

Another way you can use small structures to your tactical advantage is to set Traps within them, and then drop one or two useful loot items someplace where your enemies will see them. These items will serve as bait. Once they enter into the structure, the Trap will activate and you'll inflict damage without actually being there.

If you encounter a hut that's raised and another soldier has already built a ramp to the doorway, you know that anything that might have been inside has already been taken. There's also a chance that the enemy is still camped out inside the small structure. When it's your soldier hanging out in one of these structures, be sure to destroy the ramp after you climb up it, to cover your tracks.

These crypts make great hiding places because there is only one entrance and no windows, and the structures are made of stone. Often you'll find something worth grabbing inside. As always, watch for the glow of a chest.

Some structures you'll encounter are falling apart, but they're still worth searching. As you can see, there's a chest on top of the RV that's parked outside.

Lonely Lodge is one of the camping areas that's been a point of interest on the island for many gaming seasons. Other camping areas come and go. In addition to coming across tents and lodges, you'll see these small log cabins scattered about.

Once inside one of these small log cabins, crouch down and guard the door, so you're ready to attack an enemy who enters. You can also take a minute to use Health or Shield replenishment items you're carrying, check or rearrange your soldier's inventory (from the Inventory screen), or place one or two Traps within the cabin as booby traps that'll surprise the next soldier who enters once you leave.

Underground Mines and Tunnels

These areas include tight, narrow, and confined spaces with lots of sharp turns that you'll need to explore and fight within. You'll often need to rely on the sounds your enemies make to get an advance warning as they approach, since you often won't see them until it's too late. When navigating through these areas, keep your soldier as quiet as possible.

The thing to remember about mines and tunnels when playing Fortnite: Battle Royale is that they should be treated like hallways or narrow spaces within any other structure. These areas are filled with sharp turns, so you never know who will jump out in front of you or from behind to launch an attack.

Your best bet is to have your soldier crouch down and tiptoe through these areas in order to create the least amount of noise possible, and always keep your close-range weapon drawn and be ready to fire.

Use blind turns and narrow bottlenecks to your advantage. By positioning your soldier in the right place, you'll be able to aim and fire at enemies the moment they become visible. Try to pre-aim the gun's targeting sights exactly where you anticipate your enemy appearing, so you're ready to fire the moment he or she is spotted.

Depending on the type of close-range weapon you're using, make sure you have a good supply of ammo on hand. Most Pistols and SMGs use Light Bullets, while Shotguns use Shells (shown here). Some of the ways to gather ammo include finding it lying on the ground, within chests, as well as within Ammo Boxes, Loot Llamas, and Supply Drops. You can also collect the ammo that an enemy soldier was carrying once they've been defeated and eliminated from a match.

Just as in any close-range fighting situation, the best weapons to use include any type of Pistol, although a Legendary-rated Hand Cannon is particularly powerful. A Pump Shotgun can also pack a wallop at close range and is often preferred over any type of Pistol for close-range firefights. Another good weapon option is an SMG or Compact SMG when you're engaged in gun battles within buildings, structures, mines, or anywhere indoors.

While in tunnels or caves, for example, look for hidden rooms or chambers. Behind this wooden wall is a chest. Can you spot its glow? Even without seeing it, if you were to listen carefully, you'd hear the unique sound a chest generates when your soldier is close to it. Smash or shoot the wall to destroy it, and then open the chest and collect what's inside.

Junkyards and Storage Container Facilities Can Also Often Be Found on the Island

While exploring these areas, smashing vehicles, cargo containers, or other types of junk using your soldier's Harvesting Tool will allow you to collect resources, but you'll make a lot of noise in the process.

During just about every gaming season thus far, the island has included at least one (usually several) junkyard or storage container facility.

If you must stay on ground level, move slowly and keep your weapon drawn. While you may encounter enemies on ground level with you, they're probably newbs. The more advanced players will be attacking from above. One way to injure or eliminate your enemies on ground level in this type of terrain is to place Traps. Shown here, there's a Trap placed on the roof of a small chamber ahead. This Trap would work better, however, if it were more strategically placed and could not be seen as easily.

The easiest way to give yourself a tactical advantage in these areas is to stay as high up as possible. Climb on top of a car, junk, or cargo container pile so you can shoot at enemies below and get a better view of the whole area. Or stay on the roof of a building that overlooks the area. A third option is to build your own reinforced ramp to get your soldier as high up as possible.

Look for chests, as well as weapons, ammo, and loot items lying on top of vehicle, junk, or cargo container piles, as well as on ground level, and within the buildings that surround these areas. As always, before you start looting, make sure the area is clear of enemies.

Wide-Open Areas (Outdoors)

You're going to encounter wide-open areas within many of the labeled points of interest on the island, as well as when you're traveling in between the points of interest. Whenever possible, use your surroundings as cover. If you're in a pinch and bullets are flying toward you, you always have the option of quickly building a barrier or mini-fortress for protection and from which you can more safely launch your own attacks.

The ground level of these areas is like a maze with lots of sharp turns that you can't see around. If your enemy is above you and you're stuck on the ground, you'll definitely be at a disadvantage in terms of being able to see what's around, as well as being able to shoot at enemies above you.

Using stone (shown here) or metal, one quick and easy barrier you can build involves first creating a vertical wall tile, and then placing a ramp/stairs tile directly behind it. If you then crouch down behind the ramp, an enemy has to blast through two layers of building tiles before being able to reach your soldier.

As you're exploring the island, typically in between labeled points of interest, you'll sometimes stumble upon a campsite. While you might find one or two worthwhile items to pick up that are lying on the ground, in this case, there's an unlit Campfire near the tents.

For added protection, add sides to your barrier. This will limit visibility, but it'll help protect you from being flanked (from the left or right).

Walk up to the Campfire and light it. For every second your soldier stands near the flames, their Health meter will get a boost. This will continue until the flames burn out.

Anytime you need to travel across wide-open terrain, run (don't walk) in a zigzag pattern, and jump randomly. If you're driving in a vehicle, make quick and random turns instead of traveling in a straight line at a steady speed. If the vehicle has a Boost option, use it randomly to alter your speed and be as unpredictable as possible. A fast-moving, unpredictable target is much harder for an enemy to hit when shooting a gun or throwing explosives.

Anytime you need a quick place to hide, try crouching down in a nearby bush. This offers no protection against attacks if you're spotted, but if the bush is large enough, it'll keep you from being seen by your enemies.

During the End Game, when the safe area of the island is very small, some gamers opt to hide their soldiers in bushes. So if you can't locate an enemy that you know is close by, try shooting or tossing explosives into the nearby bushes.

If you're lucky enough to spot a rare Loot Llama out in the open and you choose to approach, do so with extreme caution. Approaching Loot Llamas without protection is something newbs often do.

On the off chance you're able to reach the Loot Llama unharmed, quickly build a brick or metal box around yourself before taking the time to collect the loot. This will offer temporary protection from an incoming attack while you open the Loot Llama and collect what's inside. This strategy also works with Supply Drops and chests that are found out in the open.

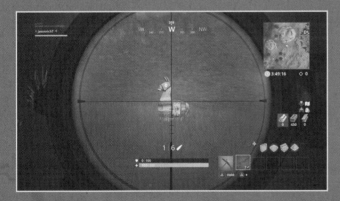

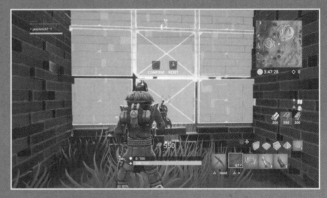

More often than not, when there's a Loot Llama or Supply Drop sitting in an open field, there's an enemy sniper hidden somewhere nearby with his Sniper Rifle targeting it. As soon as a newb approaches, he or she will be shot.

After collecting what's within the Loot Llama, simply build a door within one of the walls that surround you and make your exit. Keep your weapon drawn in case your actions have attracted some unwanted attention.

Anytime you're building a fortress or structure (especially during the End Game), don't forget to add a roof. One of the biggest mistakes newbs make is not building a roof.

When you skip adding a roof to your fortress, this gives your enemies the opportunity to toss explosives up over the walls of the fortress (or drop them down from above your fortress), so they explode in the small area where the soldiers are hiding. This is a quick way to cause mega-damage to both the structure and its inhabitants.

Shown here, Stink Bombs are being dropped from a cliff above where a soldier built a mini-fortress that has no roof. Once these bombs detonate, the soldier inside the fortress will be forced to quickly leave and can then easily be shot at and terminated.

Expect the Unexpected!

Now that you know what to expect from the terrain when exploring the island during each match, there's another extremely important thing you need to take into account—the actions of your adversaries.

Each soldier you encounter on the island is being controlled, in real time, by another gamer. He or she might be a newb, or they could be one of the highest-ranking *Fortnite: Battle Royale* gamers in the world—you just don't know unless you study their actions.

Whenever you encounter an enemy (or enemies), don't expect them to use common sense when reacting to your actions. Every gamer has their own unique style and strategies, and some have had much less practice than others when playing *Fortnite: Battle Royale*. Therefore, expect the unexpected.

Likewise, when controlling your own soldier during a match, try to be as unpredictable as possible in your movements and actions. If your enemies can't figure out what you're going to do next, they can't prepare to defend themselves against it. Be spontaneous and use the terrain around you to your utmost advantage.

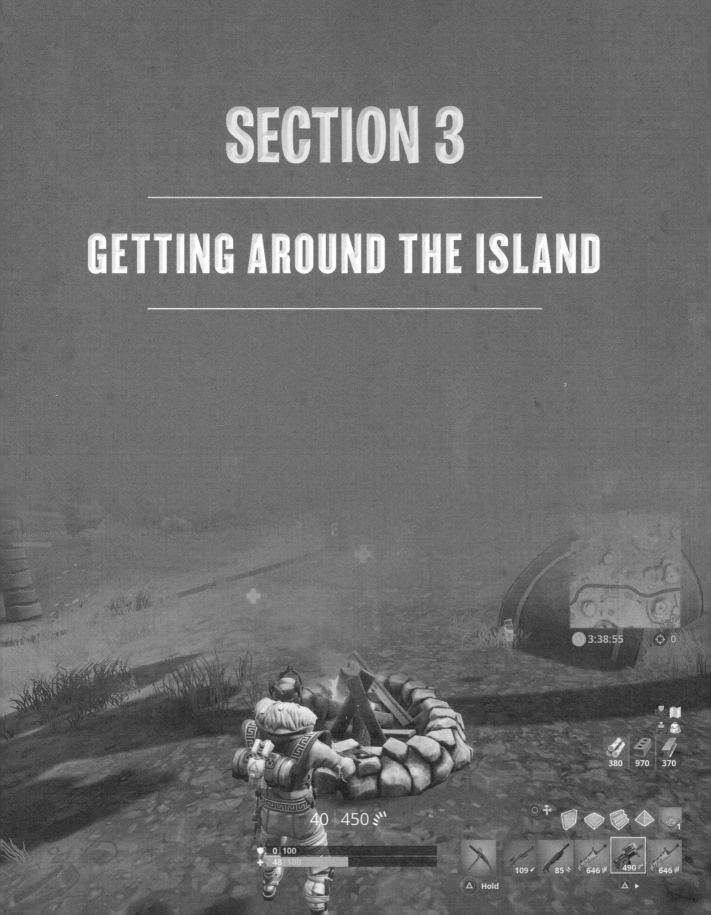

SECTION 3

GETTING AROUND THE ISLAND

Between staying away from the storm, remaining alive until the End Game, and continuously having to engage with enemies—either offensively or defensively—during every match you participate in, you'll often need to keep your soldier on the move most of the time.

During those brief times during a match when you're not outrunning the storm, and there are no enemies in the immediate vicinity, take the time to manage your soldier's inventory (from the Inventory screen).

Another practical way to spend those brief moments of rest, especially when you're able to safely hide within a structure, is to replenish your soldier's Health and/or Shields using loot items available in your inventory.

A few other ways you can enjoy your free time during a match, when there's little to no risk of being attacked, is to showcase your favorite emotes. Have your soldier break out into a dance, or use Spray Paint Tags to decorate your surroundings, for example.

If you've collected a basketball emote, look for a basketball court on the island, and play a few rounds of hoops. This offers no tactical advantage, and will not boost your player XP, but it's a fun way to pass the time. Just watch out for enemies that might sneak up and launch a surprise attack.

Health- and Shield-Related Items

The following chart offers a summary of the popular Health and Shield replenishment items that are typically available on the island. Keep in mind, new items are frequently introduced, while others get vaulted. Be sure you take full advantage of the items currently available in order to help keep your soldier healthy and battle-ready during a match.

As you'll discover, some items get stored within one of your soldier's six main inventory slots, while others can also be stored within your soldier's inventory, but in a slot found on the Inventory screen to the right of your soldier's Resources. To use them, you must first switch from Combat mode to Building mode, and then select and activate the selected item.

LOOT ITEM	HOW LONG IT TAKES TO USE OR CONSUME	POWERUP BENEFIT	STORAGE LOCATION	MAXIMUM NUMBER YOU CAN CARRY
Apples	Almost Instantly	Increases your soldier's Health meter by 5 points per Apple that's consumed.	Apples must be consumed when and where they're found (which is usually under trees). They cannot be carried and used later.	None
Bananas	Almost Instantly	Increases your soldier's Health meter by 5 points per Banana that's consumed. These items are found mainly in tropical areas.	Bananas must be consumed when and where they're found. They cannot be carried and used later.	None
Bandages	4 seconds	Increases your soldier's Health meter by 15 points.	Requires one backpack inventory slot.	15
Chug Jug	15 seconds	Replenishes your soldier's Health *and* Shield meter to 100.	Requires one backpack inventory slot.	**1**
Coconuts	Almost Instantly	Increases your soldier's Health meter by 5 points per Coconut that's consumed. However, if your soldier's Health meter is at 100, his or her Shield meter will receive some replenishment.	Coconuts must be consumed when and where they're found. They cannot be carried and used later.	None
Cozy Campfire	25 seconds	Boosts each soldier's Health HP by 2 points for every second they're standing near the flames for up to 25 seconds. If fully utilized, it boosts a soldier's Health meter by 50 points.	Stored with a soldier's resources, so it's accessed from Building mode, not Combat mode.	Unknown

(Continued on next page)

LOOT ITEM	HOW LONG IT TAKES TO USE OR CONSUME	POWERUP BENEFIT	STORAGE LOCATION	MAXIMUM NUMBER YOU CAN CARRY
Med Kits	10 seconds	Replenishes your soldier's Health meter back to 100.	Requires one backpack inventory slot.	3
Mushrooms	Almost instantly	Increases your soldier's Shield meter by 5 points (up to 100).	Mushrooms must be consumed when and where they're found. They cannot be carried and used later.	None
Peppers	Almost Instantly	Increases your soldier's Health meter by 5 points per Pepper that's consumed. Your soldier will also be able to move 20 percent faster for a short time. These items are found mainly in desert areas.	Peppers must be consumed when and where they're found. They cannot be carried and used later.	None
Shield Potion	5 seconds	Replenishes your soldier's Shield meter by 50 points (up to 100 maximum).	Requires one backpack inventory slot.	2
Slurp Juice	Approximately 2 seconds to consume and 37.5 seconds to achieve its full benefit.	A soldier's Health *and* Shield meter increases by one point (up to 75 points) for every half-second this drink is being consumed.	Requires one backpack inventory slot.	1
Small Shield Potion	2 seconds	Replenishes your soldier's Shield meter by 25 points.	Requires one backpack inventory slot.	10

Most Health and Shield replenishment items take just a few seconds to use (during which time your soldier cannot move or use a weapon). However, using items like a Cozy Campfire will take longer. While hiding out in a fortress or structure, place a Cozy Campfire on the ground, and then bask in the warmth of the flames as your soldier's Health meter gets replenished for up to 35 seconds.

You'll also discover Campfires randomly scattered on the island that your soldier can walk up to, light, and then stand near in order to replenish their health. These items can't be moved and can only be activated once per match. Once the flame burns out, the Campfire is no longer useful. Since these tend to be found in open areas (campsites), make sure the area is safe. On the plus side, you can keep your weapon in hand and be ready to fight if an enemy approaches. However, as soon as your soldier moves away from the flames, the healing effect will stop.

Learn to Switch Weapons Quickly

Either as you prepare for a firefight or while in the middle of one, there will be many times during a match when you must quickly switch between active weapons and items, or switch between Combat mode and Building mode. This is a skill that'll take practice.

Combat mode gives you full access to your weapons, loot items, and anything else in your soldier's inventory. When in Building mode, your soldier can use the resources he or she has collected (wood, stone, and metal) to build structures and fortresses. While in Building mode, however, no weapons can be used.

On most gaming systems, displayed in the bottom-right corner of the main game screen is a summary of your soldier's main inventory. Each of the slots represents one weapon or item your soldier is carrying. The leftmost slot typically contains the Harvesting Tool. This cannot be dropped.

You do have full control over the six remaining inventory slots. As you find and grab weapons and loot items, pick and choose what you want to carry and have available, and then from the Inventory screen, rearrange the order of the items as needed.

Some gamers opt to place their favorite type of gun in the slot to the immediate right of the Harvesting Tool (the slot on the extreme left). They use the next one or two slots for their next most commonly used weapons, and then insert one or two loot items (such as a Health or Shield replenishment item) in the rightmost inventory slots. (A slot for the Harvesting Tool is displayed on some gaming systems, but not others.)

Shown here, the leftmost slot contains a Suppressed Assault Rifle. To the right of it is a Burst Assault Rifle. The middle slot was reserved, in this case, for a Quad Launcher (a projectile explosive weapon), while Grenades (a throwable explosive weapon) were placed within the fourth slot. In the rightmost slot is a Slurp Juice (a Health and Shield replenishment item).

From the Inventory screen, use the Move or Drop commands to rearrange what's in each inventory slot as needed. Here, a weapon is being moved into the leftmost slot.

During firefights, keep your eye on the amount of ammo within the gun you're using. Each weapon takes a different amount of time to reload, during which time you cannot fire that weapon.

Knowing that you'll need to reload your weapon, choose an object you can duck behind for protection, such as a barrier or wall.

To speed up the time it takes once a weapon needs to be reloaded, consider having a duplicate weapon in the inventory slot next to the one you're using. When one gun needs to be reloaded, simply switch to the other one. There will still be a small amount of time where you can't shoot, but the time will often be shorter than reloading the one weapon. Shown here, there are Heavy Assault Rifles in the two leftmost inventory slots. One is rated Rare (with a blue hue) and the second is rated Common (with a gray hue).

Weapons are ranked based on color. Legendary weapons (with a gold hue) are the most powerful. Epic weapons have a purple hue, Rare weapons have a blue hue, Uncommon weapons have a green hue, and Common weapons have a gray hue. Common weapons are the least powerful.

All guns are also rated based on their DPS (Damage Per Second) rating, Damage Rate, Fire Rate, Magazine Size, and Reload Time, for example. The focus of this particular strategy guide is not on *Fortnite: Battle Royale*'s weapons.

To stay up-to-date on all of the weapons currently available within *Fortnite: Battle Royale*, and to see the ratings for each weapon, check out any of these independent websites:

- **Fortnite Weapon Stats & Info**—https://fortnitestats.com/weapons
- **Gamepedia Fortnite Wiki**—https://fortnite.gamepedia.com/Fortnite_Wiki
- **GameSkinny Fortnite Weapons List**—www.gameskinny.com/9mt22/complete-fortnite-battle-royale-weapons-stats-list
- **Metabomb**—www.metabomb.net/fortnite-battle-royale/gameplay-guides/fortnite-battle-royale-all-weapons-tier-list-with-stats-14
- **Tracker Network (Fortnite)**—https://db.fortnitetracker.com/weapons

Managing Your Soldier's Inventory

At any time during a match, an overview of your soldier's inventory is displayed on the screen. Depending on which gaming system you're using, this information is typically found near the bottom-right corner. After this soldier spent some unfortunate time in the storm, his Health meter is dangerously low (at just 5HP out of 100HP). Luckily, he stumbles upon this Med Kit to replenish his health.

The problem is that his inventory is full, so he needed to drop the Assault Rifle he was holding, grab and use the Med Kit (shown here), and then pick up the dropped weapon from the ground.

In addition to your Soldier's Harvesting Tool, which they always carry (it cannot be dropped at any time), your soldier has six inventory slots that can hold weapons or certain types of loot items (such as Health and Shield replenishment items).

As you're looking at the inventory icons displayed in the bottom-right corner of the screen, the number associated with each item tells you one of two things. If the icon relates to a weapon, it shows you how much compatible ammo you currently have for that weapon. If the icon is

for an item, it shows you how many of that item you have on hand. The weapon or item that's currently selected and active will display a yellow box around its inventory icon slot.

To see and manage your soldier's entire inventory, it's necessary to access their Inventory screen. This is done by pressing the assigned Inventory button on your keyboard/mouse or controller.

The Inventory screen displays a lot of useful information. On the top-right side of the screen, you'll see a summary of the Resources your soldier is carrying—including wood, stone, and metal. Below this, also on the right side of the screen, is a summary of the ammunition your soldier currently has on hand. Each ammo icon represents one of the five types of ammo (Light Bullets, Medium Bullets, Heavy Bullets, Shells, and Rockets), and shows how many rounds of each ammo type you have available.

Displayed to the right of your soldier's Resources on the Inventory screen (when applicable) is information about the Traps and other items (such as Cozy Campfires), that are stored in your soldier's Inventory, but that don't take up one of the six main inventory slots. To access any of these items, while viewing the main game screen, switch to Building mode using the assigned keyboard/ mouse key or controller button, and then press the keyboard key, mouse button, or controller button assigned to the additional weapons and tools.

When your soldier is holding multiple Traps or items that are not included within the six main inventory slots (when playing on a console-based gaming system), you'll need to enter into Building mode, and then keep pressing the appropriate controller button to scroll through the items in order to select the one you want to use. On a computer, each item is bound to a different keyboard key or mouse button.

Displayed in the bottom-right corner of the Inventory screen are the seven main inventory slots. On most gaming systems, the leftmost slot always holds the Harvesting Tool. On some gaming systems, the Harvesting Tool slot is not shown. It's possible to rearrange the items being held in the other six slots to make them easier to access during a match.

As you're looking at the Inventory screen, use the directional controls to highlight and select the weapon, ammo type, or item you want to access or use. The selected item's icon will display a yellow frame around in.

If you have a weapon selected, details about the weapon's category, color-coded rating, and related stats are displayed on the left side of the screen. When you're not sure how to best use a weapon or what type of ammo it requires, for example, this is a quick way to access the information.

Anytime you access your soldier's Inventory screen, this takes your attention away from the main game screen. The match does not pause, so your soldier potentially becomes vulnerable to attack.

Only access the Inventory screen when you're in a safe location (such as a small and enclosed room with the door shut). While viewing this screen, even though you can't see what's happening around your soldier, you can still hear sound effects, so pay attention to the sound of approaching enemies or nearby weapons fire. If it sounds like an enemy is approaching or you may soon be under attack, exit the Inventory screen quickly and be ready to take defensive actions!

How to Rearrange What's in Inventory Slots

Whenever you pick up a new weapon or loot item, it automatically gets placed within an available inventory slot. Your soldier's inventory slots initially fill up from left to right.

However, during a match, it's a good strategy to rearrange the items in your inventory so your most powerful and frequently used weapons and items are placed in the leftmost slots. To rearrange what's in your inventory slots, follow these steps:

- Access your soldier's Inventory screen.
- Highlight and select one of the items you want to move.
- On a PC, drag the item from one inventory slot to another. On a console-based system, select the Move command, and then position the cursor over the slot you want to move the selected item to.

In most situations, it makes little or no sense to carry around two of the same weapon, since inventory space is limited and you want to have a well-rounded selection of weapons available.

One instance when you might want to carry duplicate weapons is when you have a favorite weapon that has a small Magazine Size and slow Reload Time. By placing the two identical weapons in inventory slots directly next to each other, instead of waiting for one weapon to reload when it runs out of ammo, you can quickly switch to the other (identical weapon) and keep firing. You're often able to switch weapons faster than it takes to reload a weapon—especially if you're using a Sniper Rifle that only holds one round of ammo at a time, for example. The soldier above is carrying two Scoped Assault Rifles and two Assault Rifles, although the rarity of the duplicate weapons is different.

How to Drop and Share Weapons, Ammo, and Items

If your soldier's six inventory slots are filled up, but you find a new weapon or item you want to grab, it becomes necessary to give something up. First choose which item you want to get rid of and select it. Next, face the item you want to pick up and grab it. The item you're holding (the one you want to trade out) will be dropped, making room for the new item you want to grab.

There will be times when you might just want to drop a weapon or item that you no longer want, or when there's something that you want to share with a partner or squad mate who is standing close to your soldier. To do this, access the Inventory screen, select the item you want to drop, and the press the keyboard key, mouse button, or controller button that's associated with the Drop command.

From the Drop Items pop-up window, choose how many of that item you want to drop (share). Press the Drop button to drop that amount of the item. Press the Max button to drop the entire inventory of that item your soldier is carrying.

Instead of wasting valuable time using the Drop Items slider, after selecting an item from the Inventory screen, select the Split command to instantly drop half of the quantity of the item that's selected. For example, if you have six Heavy Bullets and you use the Split command, you'll keep three Heavy Bullets in your inventory and drop three for someone else to pick up.

Anytime you opt to Drop or Share a weapon or item, make sure an ally is nearby and picks it up. Otherwise, any soldier (including your enemies) could stumble upon what you've dropped and grab it. Sometimes, in order to pick up a more powerful or useful item, you'll need to drop a less powerful or less useful item. However, you run the risk of an enemy acquiring it.

If you want to share an item from your inventory (in this case Dynamite) and your soldier is currently carrying multiples of that item, select the item you want to share with a nearby ally, and select the Drop command (see in the bottom-right corner of the screen).

Exploring the Island on Foot

Moving from one location to the next on the island is a requirement during a match. However, getting to where you need to go on foot—whether you're walking, running, or tiptoeing, is definitely your slowest option.

During any gaming season, *Fortnite: Battle Royale* offers many different vehicles, tools, and natural phenomenon that allow you to travel around the island, and cover greater distances, must faster than if your soldier is on foot.

Examples of vehicles are a Quadcrasher, a Baller (shown here), or a Hoverboard.

During any gaming season, various natural phenomena found on the island can also help to quickly transport your soldier from one location to another. Two examples of these are Geysers and Rifts (shown above). These are part of the island, often randomly generated, and cannot be collected or moved. When you come across one of these phenomenon you can only use it when and where you find it.

Tools, like a Bounce Pad, Grappler, Balloons, or Glider can be found within chests, Loot Llamas, Supply Drops, or acquired from defeated enemies, for example. These can be used to help your soldier go airborne. Once airborne, use the directional controls to navigate.

While you're airborne, your soldier remains a moving target and can be shot. In some cases, you'll be able to shoot while in the air, but in other cases, while you're airborne, you're a vulnerable target.

Stepping onto a Geyser (shown above) or into a Rift will cause your soldier to be flung into the air. As he falls back toward land, the Glider will activate, and you'll be able to navigate rather precisely to a desired landing location.

While Rifts occur on the island as natural phenomena and appear randomly but typically within specific types of terrain (in this case desert terrain), a Rift-To-Go item can be found, added to your soldier's inventory, and then used to create a Rift anywhere and anytime it's needed. This item does take up one of your soldier's available inventory slots, however.

During the End Game, a Rift-To-Go is very handy if you need to quickly relocate or if you need to make a quick retreat from a battle.

When driving or riding in most types of vehicles, you can take advantage of the island's natural phenomenon, such as a Geyser or Rift, to transport your soldier (and the vehicle) elsewhere.

Anytime you're traveling on foot, especially if you're currently near the outskirts of the island, keep your eye on the timer (below the mini-map on the main game screen) to determine when the storm will be moving next, and then check the island map to see how far your soldier will need to travel to stay in the safe zone once the storm moves again.

Some gamers prefer to stay near the edge of the storm (on the safe side of the blue wall) as opposed to traveling around toward the center of the safe zone. Especially toward the End Game,

when the circle is small, being near the center can attract unwanted attention from other gamers. Staying along the edges of the circle helps you avoid attention and gives you a broader view of the safe area.

At this point in the match, the circle is rather small and the soldier is standing near the outer edge of the safe zone, near the blue wall, but is looking out into the region that remains safe. All the remaining soldiers in the match are somewhere within this area.

Where to Find Vehicles

Knowing where you need to travel to on the island is one thing but discovering the best way to get there is another thing altogether. That's where vehicles, certain types of loot items, and the island's natural phenomenon are extremely useful. The next several sections of this guide focus on the various ways to get around the island, as well as the best ways to use each of them.

Depending on the type of vehicle, item, or island natural phenomenon you want to use, where you'll find them will vary. Some locations are random for each match. Others are placed only in specific terrain types on the island.

In some cases, the location of a vehicle will be somewhat consistent within a specific area or terrain type, but its exact location will vary slightly from match to match. For example, during Season 8, a Baller was most commonly found in or around Expedition Outposts (one is shown here) and Pirate Camps on the island but appeared in other random locations as well.

Keep in mind, during each new gaming season, certain ways to get around the island are vaulted from *Fortnite: Battle Royale*'s Solo, Duos, and Squads matches while new ones are introduced. Vaulted vehicles may still appear in other game play modes, however.

As you play matches, remember where you spot vehicles, and then in future matches, try revisiting those locations to see if they show up again. Once you discover some location consistency, make it a priority to be the first soldier to reach that location, so you can use the vehicle before your enemies take possession or control of it.

While in some situations, which vehicle or mode of transportation you'll have access to will be dependent on your current location. Anytime you're playing a Duos or Squads match (or working with other gamers), remember that some

vehicles hold a driver, along with one, two, or three passengers at once. Thus, if you're traveling with others, you can all ride in the same vehicle.

During a Duos or Squads match, while it might make sense to travel as a group in a single vehicle in some situations, in others, you might choose to travel together, but in separate vehicles. This way, if one vehicle in the convoy gets attacked and destroyed, the driver and passenger(s) in the destroyed vehicle can hop into a secondary vehicle being driven by a squad mate.

When traveling in a separate vehicle from your partner, squad mate(s), or teammate(s), leave some space between the vehicles. This way, if one is attacked by a projectile explosive weapon, for example, the other vehicle won't get damaged.

SECTION 4

DRIVER'S EDUCATION FOR ISLAND VEHICLES

Depending on the gaming season, which *Fortnite: Battle Royale* game play mode you're experiencing, and where on the island your soldier happens to be exploring, your options for getting around the island will vary.

Of course, your soldier can always, walk, run, jump, or tiptoe around the island to get from location to location and avoid the storm, but this is not the fastest or most efficient way to travel—especially when you must cover a lot of distance quickly.

This section focuses on some of the vehicles you're likely to encounter when playing the different game play modes in *Fortnite: Battle Royale*. You'll also discover plenty of driving and navigation tips, and in some cases, learn how to use these modes of transportation to your tactical or defensive advantage.

All-Terrain Kart (ATK)

An All-Terrain Kart (also known as an ATK) is a souped-up golf cart. In addition to the driver, it can hold up to three passengers—an entire squad that wants to travel together when playing a Squads match, for example.

An ATK can travel at a moderate speed, but it's not too good on rough terrain, because it gets damaged easily. Each ATK has an HP meter that maxes out at 400HP. If it receives too much damage, it'll get destroyed.

As the driver, use the directional controls on your keyboard/controller to make the ATK move forward or backward, as well as turn left or right. There's also a horn. When playing a Duos or Squads match, some gamers use the horn to get the attention of their partner or squad mates, to inform them to jump aboard. However, the horn will attract the attention of enemies who are nearby, as will the sound of the ATK's loud engine.

Check the on-screen HUD display to see a menu of commands used to navigate and drive the vehicle. As you can see on the left side of the screen, while driving an ATK, you can Switch Seats, travel Forward, Break/Reverse, Powerslide (used to make the wheels spark so you can use the Boost feature), Honk the horn, or Exit the vehicle.

Like most vehicles, an ATK can use a Geyser or Rift to go airborne and travel a good distance while off the ground.

If you try driving up a hill or mountainside that's too steep, an ATK will make it partway up, but then slide back down, and possibly roll over. Try using the Powerslide and then Boost feature to increase the vehicle's speed before attempting to drive up a steep slope.

To quickly, but temporarily pick up speed, use the ATK's Boost feature. Hold down the Powerslide button until the rear wheels really start to spark (and turn reddish). When you release the Powerslide button, the ATK will shoot forward. It'll take some space to do this, since the Powerslide will cause the ATK to skid in circles quickly.

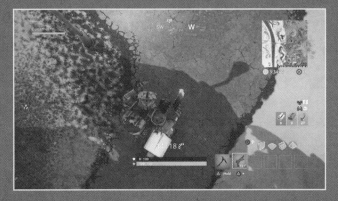

Located on the back of an ATK is a Bounce Pad. Use it to jump upward.

An ATK can travel through water, but if the water is deep, movement will be very slow.

Traveling along a river, because it's shallow, won't slow down an ATK.

If given the choice between an ATK and a Quad-crasher, always go with the Quadcrasher. It's a faster and more durable vehicle. It also has an easier-to-use Boost option that allows it to temporarily move faster.

When driving an ATK, your soldier cannot use a weapon. If an enemy starts shooting or throwing explosives, the driver will either need to stop the vehicle, jump out, and return fire, or try to evade the incoming attack and make a quick retreat. However, passengers in an ATK can use their weapons while the vehicle is in motion.

While driving an ATK, you can crash into things. Depending on the size of what gets crashed into, either the ATK will smash the object and sustain no damage, or its HP meter will take a hit.

If you flip the ATK, which isn't too hard to do, your soldier will need to exit the vehicle, face it, and then use the Flip command to turn the vehicle upright before it can be driven again.

Crashing into this large and thick tree caused the ATK to come to an abrupt stop.

You can drive an ATK off a cliff or other high point, so it goes airborne. In some cases, the vehicle might take some damage upon landing, but your soldier will not get injured.

While driving an ATK (or some other vehicles), if you spot a Loot Llama, crash right into it. This will cause the Loot Llama to burst open and reveal what's inside. You can then back up and drive over the loot to collect ammo, Traps, and certain other items without getting out of the vehicle. To grab weapons, for example, you'll need to leave the vehicle and pick them up manually.

Come to a complete stop before exiting the vehicle. Otherwise, the ATK will keep rolling forward for a few seconds. Also, when you exit the ATK, the weapon in your soldier's hands will be the one that was active when he first hopped into the vehicle. Always pre-select a weapon (before entering a vehicle) that you'll want or need to use upon exiting that vehicle. If you need to take a few extra seconds to exit and then select a weapon, that could be a fatal mistake if your soldier is already being shot at.

How to Attack a Moving Vehicle

Always listen for the sound of an approaching vehicle. You'll often hear it before you can see it. Once you spot an enemy driving a vehicle, you have four options:

1. Use your gun and start shooting. You can either aim for the driver and try to defeat them directly or aim for the vehicle and inflict as much HP damage as possible. From a distance, using a Sniper Rifle (or weapon with a scope) works nicely, but you need to take into account that the vehicle is in motion, and aim accordingly. In other words, depending on your distance from the vehicle, aim slightly in front of it.
2. Attack a vehicle using throwable explosives. A Clinger will work really well, because it'll stick onto the vehicle and then explode. A Grenade can also work, but you need to toss it into the vehicle. If the Grenade hits the outside of a vehicle, it'll often just bounce off. The same is true with other types of throwable explosives, like Dynamite.
3. Take advantage of a projectile exploding weapon, such as a Rocket Launcher, Guided Missile Launcher, or Quad Launcher. Target the vehicle and blast it with one or two direct hits. Not only will this likely destroy the vehicle, but it'll typically defeat (or at least injure) whomever is inside.
4. Avoid the vehicle altogether and allow it to pass without a confrontation.

Baller

Perhaps this vehicle was inspired by the latest Jurassic Park movies, or one of those wheels you can buy at the pet store for a hamster. Regardless of how its design was conceived, this ball-shaped vehicle is very durable, easily maneuverable, works on any type of terrain, has a built-in grappling hook, and is fun to drive.

A Baller has an HP meter that maxes out at 300HP. It can hold just one driver and no passengers, but it can roll almost anywhere and keep your soldier safe while they're inside it. Using the directional controls, a Baller can go in any direction—including up or down hills or mountains—with relative ease. It can also roll off a cliff and go airborne. When it lands, it'll typically bounce around, but receive no damage.

The Baller's grappling hook can be shot from the vehicle, latch onto another object, and then quickly draw the Baller toward that object. The more creative you are when using this tool, the more maneuverable the vehicle will be, especially if you need to reach high-up locations where the vehicle can't simply roll.

While you're driving a Baller, it can crash into or smash through almost anything, such as a rock formation, mountain, building, or structure, and receive zero damage. Likewise, your soldier will receive zero fall damage if you drive off a cliff, for example. What can damage a Baller, however, are direct hits from an enemy's weapons. But, this vehicle can withstand a lot of damage before it gets destroyed.

With practice and perfect timing, use the Baller's grappling hook to swing from tree to tree in a forest area, or use it to launch onto something overhead and pull the vehicle upward.

Unfortunately, while driving a Baller, your soldier cannot use a weapon and shoot at enemies. You can potentially crash directly into an enemy while traveling at a high speed or use the vehicle's grappling hook on them. Ballers are great for evading enemies and quickly traveling from one location to another, regardless of the terrain.

On the plus side, a Baller is much quieter than an ATK or Quadcrasher, so you can be stealthy when traveling around.

Initially (at least during Season 8), Ballers were most commonly be found near Expedition Outposts and Pirate Camps on the island, but occasionally, you'll find them elsewhere too, especially if they've been abandoned by another soldier.

Once in a while, you'll discover a Baller inside of a building or structure. In this case, you'll need to manually smash a wall to create a clearing big enough for the Baller to roll out of. Do this using your soldier's Harvesting Tool before entering the vehicle.

As a Baller's HP starts to dwindle, you'll start seeing cracks in the ball. These can't be repaired. Try to find a safe location where your soldier can exit the vehicle and then defend himself using the weapons in his arsenal. You don't want the Baller to be destroyed while you're out in the open, vulnerable to attack, with no place to take cover.

A Baller is particularly useful for outrunning the storm or escaping from it if you get caught within the storm. Keep using the Boost feature to speed up the vehicle and help you leave the storm faster so your soldier's HP suffers less damage.

Drift Board (Hoverboard)

You're able to drive a Baller up (or down) steep hills or ramps, for example, or even drive directly into a building if the entranceway is wide enough.

This is typically the fastest moving, most maneuverable type of vehicle available on the island. It works on any terrain and allows your soldier to float just above the ground.

Perhaps the best thing about a Baller is that it can go airborne by driving over a cliff, using a Rift or Geyser, or with the help of its grappling hook, yet your soldier will always land safely.

While riding a Hoverboard (also called a Drift Board), your soldier can use whatever weapon they're carrying, so you can shoot and move at the same time. Aiming and hitting targets while traveling at a high speed is relatively difficult, however.

The most awesome thing about a Hoverboard is that it's indestructible. While an enemy can shoot at your soldier and injure or defeat them, the vehicle itself will remain undamaged.

A Hoverboard can be used to outrun the storm. It can also travel almost anywhere, including up or down mountains, and directly over cliffs (so it goes airborne).

This is a one-person vehicle. However, in some locations, especially if you're playing a Duos or Squads match you'll discover multiple Hoverboards in one location, so your partner or each squad member can grab one and you can all travel together.

When following a partner, squad mate, or teammate who is riding another Hoverboard, don't follow too closely behind. Leave a little distance so you can react better to incoming attacks and make course alternations as needed, without crashing into each other or other objects.

While in motion, use the Hoverboard's Boost feature to blast your vehicle forward for a few seconds and pick up speed.

This is one of the few vehicles that you can use in conjunction with other items, such as Balloons, or a Health/Shield replenishment item. For example, when you're driving a Hoverboard and inflate two or three balloons, you can go airborne and take to the skies as you travel. You're still an open target that enemies can shoot at, and the Hoverboard will be a bit less maneuverable, but this is always an option.

A Hoverboard can also be used at the same time as an Emote (in this case, the Fire Spinner).

Like most vehicles on the island, anytime you come across a Hoverboard, you can hop on it and start driving. When you stop the Hoverboard and hop off of it, your soldier cannot pick it up, add it to their inventory, and take it with them. It'll stay where it is until you return to that location or another soldier commandeers it.

Due to its smaller size, a Hoverboard can be ridden within buildings and structures, but you'll need to travel slowly to maintain maximum navigational control to avoid constantly crashing into walls and objects that'll slow you down even more. Depending on the structure, it might make sense to park the Hoverboard near the entrance, explore and loot the building on foot, and then jump aboard the Hoverboard again when you're ready to leave and travel back outside.

Thanks to its speed and maneuverability, it can go virtually anywhere on the island, including up or down ramps, with ease. This is also a very quiet vehicle.

While airborne, do some twists, turns, and flips as you practice performing tricks.

Glider

Unlike with other vehicles, you do not need to hop off of a Hoverboard in order to open chests and collect what's inside them. You can also interact with other items, weapons, and tools you encounter.

Unlike vehicles that you'll find parked at various locations around the island, a Glider is actually a loot item that your soldier can find, pick up, add to their inventory, and then activate when it's needed.

Gliding over water, snow, or ice is quick and easy. Very little can slow down a Hoverboard. When going at medium speed, be gentle with the directional controls to maximize your maneuverability and control.

Glider items can be found lying on the ground, out in the open. They're also sometimes found within chests (shown here), Loot Llamas, and/or Supply Drops, for example, or you can pick one off of an enemy soldier whom you've defeated. You might also discover a Glider item being offered from a Vending Machine.

Glider items are a bit tricky in that they can only be used in certain circumstances. First select the item from its inventory slot. You then need to have your soldier leap off of a high location, such as a mountaintop, cliff, or building's roof. At the exact right moment, activate the Glider. Your soldier can then glide through the air, travel horizontally across a great distance (depending on the height), and then land safely. However, if your timing isn't perfect, the Glider won't open in time, and your soldier will land with a splat.

While airborne, your soldier cannot use a weapon. Use the directional controls to navigate and choose a landing location, but keep in mind that your soldier can be shot at while airborne or while landing, so you may need to take some evasive maneuvers to avoid an attack.

Like a Bouncer Pad or Launch Pad, a Glider is an ideal tool if you need to escape (or relocate) from the top of a building or fortress quickly, such as during the End Game portion of a match.

If you need to get to a high-up location quickly in order to deploy a Glider, build a tall ramp and then leap off of it.

When Glider items are available during matches, they tend to be pretty common. They do, however, take some practice to use effectively

and safely. Once you collect a Glider item, it can only be deployed 10 times before it disappears from your soldier's inventory.

Once a Glider is deployed successfully, control it the same ways as you'd control your soldier's Glider during freefall after leaving the Battle Bus at the start of a match. Whichever Glider design you've selected for your soldier before a match will be the one that's used during the match in conjunction with the Glider item. All Glider designs function exactly the same way. The differences in appearance are cosmetic only.

Quadcrasher

Out of all the vehicles offered on the island, a Quadcrasher is probably the most durable, maneuverable, and versatile. It can travel across any type of terrain—including through water. It's HP meter maxes out at 500HP, so it can take a lot of damage before it's destroyed.

Unlike an ATK, it's very difficult to damage a Quadcrasher while driving it. Crashing into objects may slow it down, but it'll cause no damage to the vehicle. As long as your soldier remains within the vehicle, he too will receive no fall damage.

As its name suggests, a Quadcrasher, which holds a driver and plus one passenger can crash through objects. The faster it's going, the larger the object it can smash through.

Use the directional controls on the keyboard/mouse or controller to go in virtually any direction, including up, down, left, right, or directly over cliffs or ramps (in order to go airborne).

The Quadcrasher has a built-in Boost feature that takes a few seconds to recharge in between uses. With each boost, the rocket in the back of the vehicle ignites, and the Quadcrasher shoots forward at an ultra-fast speed. Use this to smash through larger objects, drive up a particularly steep hill, or to travel faster along flat terrain.

A Quadcrasher can also drive up a ramp and use it as a jump to go airborne for a few seconds. The landing will always be safe. Of course, it can also climb some steep hills and rock formations.

While it's difficult to destroy or even damage a Quadcrasher by driving it, these vehicles can be damaged or destroyed by incoming gunfire or explosive weapon attacks. They also make a lot of noise, so they can be heard approaching from a distance.

It is possible to crash directly into an enemy. They'll go flying backward but won't be badly injured. However, if you crash into a building, structure, or object, especially when using the vehicle's Boost feature, chances are you'll smash right through it and destroy whatever you crash into.

Prior to a match, access the Locker and select a Vehicle Wrap to customize the appearance of most vehicles, including a Quadcrasher. Vehicle Wraps can be purchased from the Item Store or unlocked by completing challenges, for example.

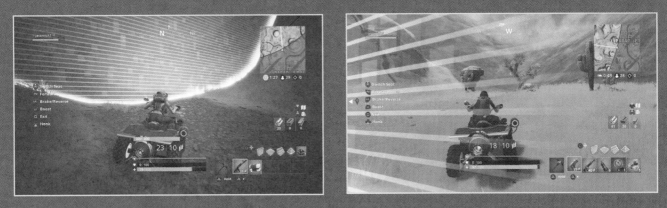

A Quadcrasher is the perfect vehicle for quickly outrunning the storm, because it moves really fast and can go virtually anywhere.

If you happen to flip over a Quadcrasher or ATK, you'll need to exit out of the vehicle, face it, and then press the Flip button on your keyboard/controller in order to reposition the vehicle upright. You can then hop back in and start driving. A vehicle typically flips over as a result of a weird landing.

When they're available within the game, Quadcrashers can be found throughout the island. They're often parked along streets in urban areas, on or near trailers parked almost anywhere (shown on the left), or within the garages attached to some homes or structures (shown on the right), for example.

Before existing a Quadcrasher (or any vehicle for that matter) first come to a complete stop. Otherwise, your soldier will jump off the vehicle, but the vehicle will keep moving forward for a few seconds.

If you try driving up a steep slope (such as a rock mountain) and the Quadcrasher loses traction and starts slipping downward, hit the Boost button.

To practice your driving skills, head for the racetrack (located near map coordinates J6). If it's no longer there, take a Quadcrasher for a spin along any open terrain, or follow some roadways. During a match, be ready to press the Boost button to blast away from an enemy that's starts shooting.

A Quadcrasher can travel through water, but if it's deep, your travel speed will be slowed down, and you could wind up being an easy target for nearby enemies—especially if they're armed with a Sniper Rifle (or other weapon with a scope) or a projectile explosive weapon, such as a Rocket Launcher, Grenade Launcher, Quad Launcher, or Boom Bow.

Depending on the gaming season and which vehicles are available, you can discover the locations where they commonly spawn on the map using your favorite Internet search engine (such as Google, Yahoo!, or Bing). Within the Search field, enter, "Fortnite [insert vehicle name] locations," and you'll discover websites that publish up-to-date maps that show vehicle locations.

SECTION 5

OTHER WAYS TO GET AROUND THE ISLAND

Sure, they're convenient when you can locate them, but vehicles are not the only way to get around the island faster than on foot. From gaming season to season, Epic Games introduces loot items and natural phenomenon to the island that can also be used to travel.

Let's take a closer look at some of these options—not all of which are available on the island when playing a Solo, Duos, or Squads match, but typically are available when playing other types of matches or different game play modes, such as Creative or Playground.

Balloons

Once you add Balloons to your soldier's inventory (they take up one inventory slot), at any time you can activate one, two, or three balloons at the same time. One Balloon is shown here. When a Balloon is strapped onto your soldier's back, any time they jump, they'll go higher and travel farther, but slowly.

Balloons are a loot item. They can be found within chests, lying on the ground (out in the open), within Loot Llamas, in Supply Drops, and are sometimes offered by Vending Machines.

Activate two Balloons at once, and your soldier will be able to jump extra high. This is useful if you need to go from ground level to the top of a tall building or mountain, for example. While airborne, use the directional controls to move your soldier around and cover more distance (in addition to going up and down).

Each time you pick up a Balloons item, it contains ten Balloons that your soldier can carry and then use as needed. Once the stash of Balloons has been used up, this item disappears from your soldier's inventory and frees up a slot.

Anytime you activate three Balloons at the same time, your soldier automatically floats upwards . . . and keeps going up . . . until you pop one or more of the Balloons or your soldier reaches a maximum possible elevation. At the same time, use the directional controls to move around. Using multiple Balloons allows you to reach high-up locations, or travel great distances while airborne, but the travel time is slow compared to other transportation options. On the plus side, using Balloons generates no noise.

With three Balloons on your soldier's back, you'll fly very high up. Once you reach a certain altitude, however, one Balloon will automatically pop, so your soldier will level off. Use the directional controls to proceed to your desired destination. While up very high, you should be out of range from most (but not all) enemy weapons. An enemy with good aim and a Sniper Rifle will still be able to pick you off, even if you're up very high.

One drawback to Balloons is that they're brightly colored and can be seen by enemies from a distance. They don't make any noise, however. While airborne, it's possible to use any of your soldier's weapons, so you can shoot in a downward direction at your enemies, but they can shoot back.

If an enemy pops all of your soldier's Balloons and he's high up in the air, he'll come crashing down to the ground and perish. So, if you have good aim and are comfortable using the weapon(s) in your soldier's arsenal, using Balloons while enemies are nearby is fine. However, if you're a newb, save this item for when enemies are not nearby and there's little risk of your soldier getting shot down.

It's possible to travel around the island on the ground and always wear one Balloon. This, of course, is literally putting a brightly-colored target on your back, but it allows your soldier to leap higher and farther anytime when using the Jump command.

When your soldier wears Balloons and uses a Hoverboard, for example, he can float through the air or glide along the ground's surface. Talk about having options!

While airborne, to travel back down toward land, pop one Balloon at a time. If you're using three Balloons to float high up in the air but pop all three at once while still high up, you'll freefall back to land and perish. When using three Balloons, pop one, drift down a bit, and then pop the second. Wait to pop the third until you're very close to land or have safely landed. When using one or two Balloons at once, the downward directional control can be used to help your soldier land, but it'll be a slow descent. Since they were first introduced, Balloons have been vaulted in some game play modes, but could be re-introduced at anytime.

Cannons

Cannons were introduced in conjunction with a pirate theme. They'll likely be vaulted after Season 9 when playing Solo, Duos, or Squads matches, but could re-appear at any time. You're probably thinking that Cannons are weapons, which is true. However, they're also on wheels and can be pushed or ridden around by a soldier.

Cannons are large, heavy, and slow moving when going up hills, but once they're at the top of a hill, they can be pushed down and ridden by one or two soldiers. As a "vehicle," Cannons function almost exactly like Shopping Carts, but they're also able to shoot cannonballs that are capable of destroying buildings, structures, and fortresses.

As a vehicle, Cannons are not too practical, especially during a Solo, Duos, or Squads match when your soldier needs to move around quickly. If you're playing any type of 50v50 match, Cannons are much more useful. You can push or ride them toward enemy territory (while being protected by teammates) and then blast away enemy strongholds.

The Grappler can be used to quickly reach the roof of houses or some other buildings and structures or, with practice, can be used to swing in the air from one target to the next, like Spider-Man®. To accomplish this, however, takes perfect aim and timing.

Grappler

Each time you pick up a Grappler item, it includes ten shots. After each shot, it takes approximately 1.3 seconds for the item to reload before it can be shot again. Once all of the shots are used up, the item disappears from your soldier's inventory. Like most items, it can be found on the ground (out in the open), within chests, within Loot Llamas, within Supply Drops, and occasionally within Vending Machines.

A Grappler is a loot item that can be found, picked up, and carried in your soldier's inventory until it's needed.

Geysers

When you select this item (after collecting it), your soldier holds and aims it like a gun. However, when targeting a solid object, such as a tree, rooftop, or building the grappling hook shoots forward, latches onto its target, and then immediately pulls your soldier toward the target.

These are a natural phenomenon that appear on the island randomly. They're also referred to as Volcano Vents. When your soldier steps on one, he'll be catapulted into the air. Use the directional arrows to navigate and choose a safe landing location. Expect the Glider to deploy automatically to ensure a safe landing.

Whether or not Geysers will remain on the island after Season 9 is anyone's guess, but if you're traveling in between points of interest on foot and have a long way to go, stepping on a Geyser can speed up your journey.

Launch Pad

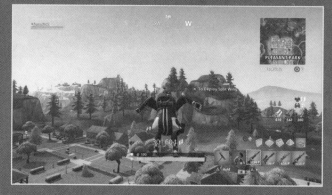

A Launch Pad is a loot item that can be found, collected, stored in inventory, and then used when it's needed to quickly catapult your soldier into the air.

Once airborne, use the directional controls to navigate as your soldier falls back toward land. Their Glider will automatically deploy to ensure a safe landing. This is a useful tool for quickly reaching the top of a mountain, house, building, or structure.

Especially during the End Game, gamers often place a Launch Pad within their fortress, so they can make a quick escape or relocate to another position if their fortress gets attacked or they need to avoid the storm.

Here, a Launch Pad has been placed on a flat surface. It's now ready to use simply by stepping on it. The drawback to using this item is its setup time. If you're in a massive hurry, it's not always practical. Plus, if an enemy is following you, they can use the same Launch Pad right after you.

A Launch Pad must be positioned on a flat surface. This often requires a solider to first build a floor tile (made of wood, stone, or metal) and then place the Launch Pad on top of it. Once it's been activated, it cannot be packed up and relocated. It can, however, be used an infinite number of times by any soldier, unless it's manually destroyed.

If you attempt to place a Launch Pad on a non-flat surface, its outline will turn red and you won't be able to active it.

Unlike many loot items, a Launch Pad gets stored within your soldier's inventory with their resources (wood, stone, and metal) and ammo. Therefore, it does not require an inventory slot. To select and activate a Launch Pad, your soldier must enter into Building mode, and then select the Launch Pad from the resources inventory. Select, position, and activate it as you would a Trap.

Rifts

Rifts are a natural phenomenon on the island. They appear semi-randomly (but usually in the same general areas of the island). When your soldier walks into a Rift, he gets catapulted into the air.

Once your soldier is airborne, use the directional controls to navigate toward the desired landing spot. The Glider will automatically deploy to ensure a safe landing. While Rifts were once rather commonplace on the island, as of Season 8, they began to appear less frequently. Their locations are random, but you might find one somewhere near the Now Entering Paradise sign as you enter/exit Paradise Palms or while exploring the desert area of the island.

Rift-To-Go

A Rift-To-Go item works exactly like a Rift, but it can be found, collected, and stored in your soldier's inventory (within an inventory slot). It can be used whenever and wherever it's needed. Each Rift-To-Go item can only be used once. It is possible to carry up to two Rift-To-Go items at the same time within the same inventory slot.

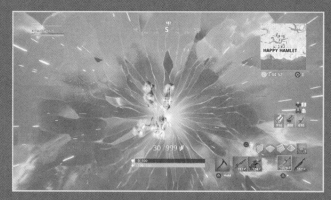

Once activated, your soldier will go airborne. Use the directional controls to navigate to another location. To ensure a safe landing, your soldier's Glider will automatically deploy. This is a useful item if you need to make a quick escape or retreat during a battle, or if you need to cover a lot of territory fast in order to outrun the storm.

Once a Rift-To-Go is activated, the Rift it creates remains open for about ten seconds. This means that other soldiers—a partner, squad mates, or even your enemies, can follow you into the Rift your soldier creates. This can be useful if you want to travel with your squad, but it can be a hinderance if you're trying to escape from an enemy and they simply follow you through the Rift.

Shopping Carts

Before ATKs and other vehicles were added to Fortnite: Battle Royale, Shopping Carts were the only type of vehicle in the game. They're not too practical and have since been vaulted, but occasionally get re-introduced within the game (for specific types of matches or game play modes).

Now that Epic Games has introduced so many other transportation options into Fortnite: Battle Royale, even if you do come across a Shopping Cart on the island, there's seldom any benefit to using it–unless you just want to push it around and have some fun.

X-4 Stormwing Airplanes

A Shopping Cart can be found randomly on the island. Your soldier can push it around. If it's positioned at the top of a hill, ramp, or mountain, for example, a soldier can then hop onto the cart and ride it.

Up to two soldiers can "ride" a Shopping Cart at once. The person pushing the cart cannot use a weapon at the same time, but a passenger can. One drawback to a Shopping Cart is that it has no brakes, so if you're traveling fast down a hill, you can't just stop.

These airplanes made a brief appearance in Fortnite: Battle Royale and allowed soldiers to take to the air and participate in mid-air battles or use the aircraft's weapons to target enemies on the ground. The X-4 Stormwing airplanes have since been vaulted from most game play modes but can still be used in the game's Creative mode, for example.

Ziplines

Crisscrossing certain regions of the island is a network of Ziplines. To ride a Zipline, walk up to one end of it, look up, and press the Enter Zipline button on your keyboard or controller. Your soldier will quickly sail through the air to the opposite end of the Zipline.

While riding a Zipline, enemies can shoot at your soldier from the ground. However, he's able to shoot back while in motion. Any time you're riding a Zipline, have a mid-range weapon in hand—preferably one with a large Magazine and quick Reload Time—and be ready to shoot.

Once you latch onto a Zipline that goes up and down a hill or mountain, your soldier can travel in either direction, as often as he wishes.

As your soldier is riding a Zipline, use the directional controls to rotate around so your soldier can look or aim his weapon in different directions. It's also possible to slow down and stop the ride at any point, and even switch directions. (The direction your soldier is facing, related to the Zipline, is the direction he'll travel.) This can be useful if you're trying to shoot at an enemy below. It's always harder to accurately shoot at a moving target, so by stopping your soldier's travel along the Zipline, it may become easier to make a shot. However, as a non-moving target, this also makes it easier for your enemies to shoot at your soldier.

When a Zipline is not too far from the ground, if you want to exit the ride early, press the Jump button and your soldier will immediately fall to the ground. This can cause an injury (or be fatal) depending on the height, so be careful! At the end of a Zipline's route, your soldier will automatically jump off safely at the landing location.

Ziplines provide a way to quickly move from one location to another. When structures are located on either end of a Zipline route, such as Expedition Outposts, these often contain useful goodies worth grabbing, so take the time to explore the huts and structures.

Ziplines were first introduced during Season 7, but they stuck around during Season 8, and will likely remain a viable mode of transportation on the island for a while. While riding any other type of vehicle, a soldier can't also ride a Zipline. However, at any time, any number of soldiers can hop onto the same Zipline at once.

If two soldiers are traveling on the same Zipline but in opposite directions, when they collide, both will fall to the ground. The red poles that hold up the Ziplines cannot be destroyed, so don't bother trying.

At the start of season 9, a network of Slipstreams was added to certain parts of the island. It's possible for a soldier to ride these air tunnels to get from one location to another.

SECTION 6

FORTNITE: BATTLE ROYALE RESOURCES

On YouTube (www.youtube.com), Twitch.TV (www.twitch.tv/directory/game/Fortnite), or Facebook Watch (www.facebook.com/watch), in the Search field, enter the search phrase *"Fortnite: Battle Royale"* to discover many game-related channels, live streams, and prerecorded videos that'll help you become a better player.

Also, be sure to check out the following online resources related to *Fortnite: Battle Royale*:

WEBSITE OR YOUTUBE CHANNEL NAME	DESCRIPTION	URL
Best *Fortnite* Settings	Discover the custom game settings used by some of the world's top-rated *Fortnite: Battle Royale* players.	www.bestfortnitesettings.com
Corsair	Consider upgrading your keyboard and mouse to one that's designed specifically for gaming. Corsair is one of several companies that manufacturers keyboards, mice, and headsets specifically for gamers.	www.corsair.com
Epic Game's Official Social Media Accounts for *Fortnite: Battle Royale*	Visit the official Facebook, Twitter, and Instagram Accounts for *Fortnite: Battle Royale*.	Facebook: www.facebook.com /FortniteGame Twitter: https://twitter.com /fortnitegame Instagram: www.instagram.com/fortnite
Fandom's *Fortnite* Wiki	Discover the latest news and strategies related to *Fortnite: Battle Royale*.	http://fortnite.wikia.com/wiki /Fortnite_Wiki
FantasticalGamer	A popular YouTuber who publishes *Fortnite* tutorial videos.	www.youtube.com/user /FantasticalGamer
FBR Insider	The *Fortnite: Battle Royale Insider* website offers game-related news, tips, and strategy videos.	www.fortniteinsider.com
Fortnite Config	An independent website that lists the custom game settings for dozens of top-rated *Fortnite: Battle Royale* players.	https://fortniteconfig.com
Fortnite Gamepedia Wiki	Read up-to-date descriptions of every weapon, loot item, and ammo type available within *Fortnite: Battle Royale.* This Wiki also maintains a comprehensive database of soldier outfits and related items released by Epic Games.	https://fortnite.gamepedia.com /Fortnite_Wiki

(Continued on next page)

WEBSITE OR YOUTUBE CHANNEL NAME	DESCRIPTION	URL
Fortnite Intel	An independent source of news related to *Fortnite: Battle Royale*.	www.fortniteintel.com
Fortnite Scout	Check your personal player stats, and analyze your performance using a bunch of colorful graphs and charts. Also check out the stats of other *Fortnite: Battle Royale* players.	www.fortnitescout.com
Fortnite Skins	This independent website maintains a detailed database of all *Fortnite: Battle Royale* outfits and accessory items released by Epic Games.	https://fortniteskins.net
Fortnite Stats & Leaderboard	This is an independent website that allows you to view your own *Fortnite*-related stats or discover the stats from the best players in the world.	https://fortnitestats.com
Fortnite: Battle Royale for Android Mobile Devices	Download *Fortnite: Battle Royale* for your compatible Android-based mobile device.	www.epicgames.com/fortnite/en-US /mobile/android/get-started
Fortnite: Battle Royale Mobile (iOS App Store)	Download *Fortnite: Battle Royale* for your Apple iPhone or iPad.	https://itunes.apple.com/us/app /fortnite/id1261357853
Game Informer Magazine's *Fortnite* Coverage	Discover articles, reviews, and news about *Fortnite: Battle Royale* published by *Game Informer* magazine.	www.gameinformer.com/fortnite
Game Skinny Online Guides	A collection of topic-specific strategy guides related to *Fortnite*.	www.gameskinny.com/tag/ fortnite-guides
GameSpot's *Fortnite* Coverage	Check out the news, reviews, and game coverage related to *Fortnite: Battle Royale* that's been published by GameSpot.	www.gamespot.com/fortnite
IGN Entertainment's *Fortnite* Coverage	Check out all IGN's past and current coverage of *Fortnite*.	www.ign.com/wikis/fortnite
Jason R. Rich's Websites and Social Media	Learn about additional, unofficial game strategy guides by Jason R. Rich that cover *Fortnite: Battle Royale*, *PUBG*, and *Apex Legends* (each sold separately).	www.JasonRich.com www.GameTipBooks.com Twitter: @JasonRich7 Instagram: @JasonRich7
Microsoft's Xbox One *Fortnite* Website	Learn about and acquire *Fortnite: Battle Royale* if you're an Xbox One gamer.	www.microsoft.com/en-US/store/p /Fortnite-Battle-Royalee/BT5P2X999VH2

WEBSITE OR YOUTUBE CHANNEL NAME	DESCRIPTION	URL
MonsterDface YouTube and Twitch.tv Channels	Watch video tutorials and live game streams from an expert *Fortnite* player.	www.youtube.com/user/MonsterdfaceLive www.Twitch.tv/MonsterDface
Ninja	On YouTube and Twitch.tv, check out the live and recorded game streams from Ninja, one of the most highly skilled *Fortnite: Battle Royale* players in the world. His YouTube channel has more than 22 million subscribers.	YouTube: www.youtube.com/user/NinjasHyper Twitch: https://twitch.tv/Ninja
Official Epic Games YouTube Channel for *Fortnite: Battle Royale*	The official *Fortnite: Battle Royale* YouTube channel.	www.youtube.com/user/epicfortnite
Pro Game Guides	This independent website maintains a detailed database of all *Fortnite: Battle Royale* outfits and accessory items released by Epic Games.	https://progameguides.com/fortnite/fortnite-features/fortnite-battle-royale-outfits-skins-cosmetics-list
ProSettings.com	An independent website that lists the custom game settings for top-ranked *Fortnite: Battle Royale* players. This website also recommends optional gaming accessories, such as keyboards, mice, graphics cards, controllers, gaming headsets, and monitors.	www.prosettings.com/game/fortnite www.prosettings.com/best-fortnite-settings
SCUF Gaming	This company makes high-end, extremely precise, customizable wireless controllers for the console-based gaming systems, including the SCUF Impact controller for the PS4. If you're looking to enhance your reaction times when playing *Fortnite: Battle Royale*, consider upgrading your wireless controller.	www.scufgaming.com
Turtle Beach Corp.	This is one of many companies that make great quality, wired or wireless (Bluetooth) gaming headsets that work with all gaming platforms.	www.turtlebeach.com

Your **Fortnite: Battle Royale** *Adventure Continues . . .*

There are dozens of reasons why more than 125 million gamers from around the world love *Fortnite: Battle Royale*, and as soon as you start playing, you'll discover all these reasons for yourself.

However, if there's one thing you need to know about this game, it's that the folks at Epic Games are working really hard to continuously release game updates and patches that allow the island and everything you encounter on it to evolve.

Be sure to visit www.epicgames.com/fortnite/en-US/news often to stay up-to-date on what's new within the game. To learn about additional unofficial strategy guides in this *Fortnite: Battle Royale Master Combat* series, visit: www.FortniteGameBooks.com.

Combine the island's geographic evolution with the constant release of new cosmetic items (Outfits, Back Bling designs, Harvesting Tool designs, emotes, etc.), powerful new weapons, and innovative new loot items, and you can expect to experience something unique almost every time you play any game play mode in *Fortnite: Battle Royale.*

Each game play mode offers its own exciting set of challenges. And of course, during each match you participate in, you'll need to outfight, outthink, and outperform up to 99 other gamers, since that's what a good Battle Royale game is all about!

Regardless of your age or your gaming skills when playing other battle royale games, keep in mind that becoming good enough at playing *Fortnite: Battle Royale* to achieve #1 Victory Royale is going to take a lot of practice! Strategies guides will help you better understand the game, but practice will help you hone your skills and win.

As you participate in each match, remember where things are, learn from your mistakes, discover what tips you can from other gamers, keep calm, and don't allow yourself to get frustrated.

Good luck, and most importantly, have fun!